Behold, I Am Coming Soon

Wycliffe Studies in Gospel, Church, and Culture

General Editor: Thomas P. Power

The series entitled Wycliffe College Studies in Gospel, Church, and Culture is intended to present topical subject matter in an accessible form and seeks to appeal to a broad audience. Typically, titles in the series derive from sermons given by the faculty of Wycliffe College, Toronto, in its Founders' Chapel. The current volume on Revelation is the sixth in the series and derives from a sermon series given in the Winter of 2018.

Behold, I Am Coming Soon

Meditations on the Apocalypse of John

EDITED BY

Mari Leesment

WIPF & STOCK · Eugene, Oregon

BEHOLD, I AM COMING SOON
Meditations on the Apocalypse of John

Wycliffe Studies in Gospel, Church, and Culture

Wipf & Stock
An Imprint of Wipf and Stock Publishers
199 W. 8th Ave., Suite 3
Eugene, OR 97401

www.wipfandstock.com

PAPERBACK ISBN: 978-1-5326-5020-8
HARDCOVER ISBN: 978-1-5326-5021-5
EBOOK ISBN: 978-1-5326-5022-2

Manufactured in the U.S.A.   11/30/18

Contents

Introduction

MARI LEESMENT

THIS BOOK CONTAINS TWELVE meditations on the New Testament (NT) book of Revelation, written by theologians, biblical scholars, historians, and clergy. In short, easy-to-read selections that are also profound and relevant to life, the meditations in this volume, along with three or four questions that accompany each meditation, help the reader engage more deeply with the Scripture passage. I believe these meditations are especially helpful since they deal with the challenges readers may face with this particular book of the Bible. Of all the books in the NT, Revelation can seem the most alien to our sensibilities. At best, it may simply be difficult to wholeheartedly embrace—difficult to get a handle on, with little that is familiar to hold onto and some ideas and images that seem entirely opaque. At worst, the scenes of violence and vengeance may seem to contradict our sense of Christian theology.

For a long time, my own experience of reading Revelation was ambivalent. However much I enjoyed certain passages, I could not understand the reason for the pages and pages of slaughter, plagues, battles, beasts, and devils. So, my reading of Revelation was limited to a selection of passages: the relatively easy to understand (and swallow) letters to the churches (Rev 2–4) and the grand scenes familiar to many churches—the ceaseless "Holy, holy, holy is the Lord God almighty, who was, who is, and who is to come" (Rev 4:8) of the angels and the congregation and the emotion-provoking twenty-four elders falling and "cast[ing] their crowns before the throne, singing, 'You are worthy . . . '" (Rev 4:10). Occasionally, I would hurry past the pages of violent wrath to the passage in Revelation 21:3–4, "God himself will be with them; he will wipe every tear from their eyes. Death will be no more; mourning and crying and pain will be no more . . . " Such glorious scenes—how could a reader of those passages not suspect there was more to this book?

I am eager for people to read the meditations in this volume because my own thinking was changed by the perspective of a teacher, and I think these meditations have potentially the same effect. For my part, I began to more fully appreciate the book of Revelation in a seminary New Testament Introduction class taught by Dr. Ian Scott. I will describe what changed, even though I will partially overlap with what is said in the meditations that follow, and with the qualification that I am likely representing my own realization, rather than accurately representing the emphases and nuances of the class lectures.

For me, the scenes of the book of Revelation that I found difficult to read and accept became more meaningful when I took seriously the circumstances of the writer and his intended readers, or more likely, hearers. The first chapter states that it records the experiences of John, when he was on Patmos, who is "sharing with you in Jesus the persecution" (Rev 1:9). Thus, John identifies his audience, describing the experience shared between him and his readers of being persecuted in the name of Jesus. Throughout the book are other indications that these are the intended audience of John's text: encouragement to remain faithful in persecution (Rev 2:8–11) and references to martyrs (Rev 16:5; 17:6), who are depicted as asking for vengeance (Rev 6:10–11, 8:9–11). Although I think Revelation could also serve as a message provoking the wealthy and powerful who oppress and persecute others to repent, the intended audience of Revelation appears to be those who are suffering or expect to suffer at their hands, like John.

To recognize that the hearer or reader of Revelation is experiencing persecution shapes our reading. In fact, Elizabeth Schüssler Fiorenza argues that inhabiting this perspective is necessary for reading Revelation correctly. Stating that a proper reading of the text requires "a jail-house" perspective, she goes on to say that the book of Revelation 'can only be understood by those "who hunger and thirst for justice."'[1] Scenes that depict the violent judgment of powerful, wealthy persecutors make more sense when they are read from the perspective of those who are powerless, poor, and oppressed, who, hemmed in, beaten down, and feeling incapable of effecting any positive change in their circumstances, despair at the idea that injustice will ever be righted.

The book of Revelation became even more meaningful when I learned that it was an apocalypse—the book describes itself as an *apokalypsis* in Greek (Rev 1:1)—a word that means "uncovering." But I also discovered that this book, called the "Apocalypse of John," in all its strangeness, was similar to other texts. Within the period corresponding to early Christianity, there were a number of Jewish and Christian texts—some also explicitly called apocalypses—that contained similar elements, like visions, beasts, symbols, vision guides, and an interplay between

---

1. Schüssler Fiorenza, *The Book of Revelation*, 198.

the spiritual and earthly realms.[2] Having embraced the
Apocalypse of John as a text that uses rhetorical strategies
that seem less strange within the context of similar texts, I
was able to read the text as a whole and consider its effect
on the audience.[3] What might be the effect of reading a text
full of fantastic beasts and devils and angels, lakes of fire,
even God himself and the heavenly realm?

Like other apocalyptic texts, John's apocalypse introduces a dual worldview, so that those who read this vision
hold together the world they know alongside the spiritual
reality. The Apocalypse of John intersperses scenes of the
earthly worship of the devil and the beast—likely referring
to emperor worship—alongside scenes of the heavenly
worship of the slain lamb. Likewise, the city of Babylon—likely representing the seat of power in the Roman
Empire, Rome—is displayed alongside a vision of the New
Jerusalem, offering a vision of an ultimate reality where
justice and true peace prevail. The apparent global empire
of Rome—the multitude of tribes, nations, and tongues
that appears to be ruled by a great and powerful ruler—is
set below (in space and ultimately in capability) God and
the multitude whose number cannot be counted (Rev
7:9). Finally, the linear narrative concluding with the fall
of the beast (Rev 19:17–21) and the earthly Babylon that
ultimately is "no more" (Rev 18: 21–24) is set alongside the
ceaseless worship by those who live eternally of the "one

2. For a good overview, see Collins, *Apocalypse, Prophecy, and
Pseudepigraphy*.

3. I am not suggesting that John's apocalypse is not the result of a
visionary experience. For my part, I think the fact that it is a vision
of heaven, and of God, explains its strangeness and that it is beyond
complete comprehension. However, I think that his thinking is constructed by the theological and religious context as can be seen in the
other apocalyptic texts of the period, and this context partially shapes
how John interpreted and described his experience.

who is and was and is coming" (Rev 1:4, 8 and 22:7, 12; cf. 3:11, 14:6–7, 16:15).[4]

Setting these alongside one another unsettles the apparent reality. As deSilva writes, the repeated scenes of the lamb on the heavenly throne are"reinforcing the Judaeo-Christian view of reality" and "[d]econstructing Roman imperial ideology."[5] John's apocalypse describes the spiritual realities, and the narrative of the final end of the devil and his servants, and so encourages the persecuted and those expecting to be martyred. If we imagine the reader with a "jail-house perspective," whose certainty in the reality of Christ's kingdom may be shaken by the visibly present kingdom of Rome, we can see that the Apocalypse of John is assuring readers that however convincing are the earthly powers, things are not as they appear. Central to John's Apocalypse appears to be a question that is arguably central to all apocalypses, "Who is Lord over this world?"[6] The scenes of the heavenly throne and the narrative that describes that "the kingdom of the world has become the

4. Recognizing at least a general narrative structure helps us to see the overarching ideas: the text involves the churches in a cosmic narrative where the kingdom of this world will come to an end and God will reign over the New Jerusalem. I agree with the structure offered by Mangina, *Revelation*, 32: epilogue (1:1–3), letters (1:4–3:22), shift in 4:1 with a climax at 11:15–17 with the statement "The kingdom of the world has become the kingdom of our Lord." Then follows a narrative of the end of this world from 12:1 to 20:15. Finally, the vision of the New Jerusalem and the marriage supper of the lamb (21:1–22:7) and epilogue (Rev 22:8–21). This structure is partially based upon that found in Barr, *Tales of the End*. See Mangina for a threefold interpretation of Jesus, with the sections describing Jesus as prophet, priest, and king.

5. DeSilva, *An Introduction to the New Testament*, 916.

6. Schüssler Fiorenza, *The Book of Revelation,* 24. She frames it as the central question of apocalyptic work: "The apocalyptic question 'Who is Lord over the world?' is the central issue of Rev."

kingdom of our Lord" (Rev 11:15) encourages the down-trodden to recognize the reality of the lamb of God on the throne. I invite you to read through the twelve meditations in this volume and be encouraged, just as those who heard it over 2,000 years ago were encouraged.

Description of the Meditations

The first meditation in this volume, written by Joseph Mangina, and called "An Encounter with the Living One: Revelation and the Healing Invasion of God," lays some groundwork for reading the Apocalypse of John. Here, in the first chapter, we recognize John's words as spoken to us, along with understanding the multiple genres of the book—prophecy, letter, apocalypse, and a revelation of Jesus.

The second meditation, by Terry Donaldson, about the letters to the seven churches in Revelation 2–3, describes "Babylon, the New Jerusalem and the Cities in between." This nuanced reading positions the multiple cities addressed by name in relation to the archetypal cities of Babylon and the New Jerusalem, and we begin to position our own cities in relation to the two final cities.

In "'Come up Here': A Glimpse of Heaven," through Marion Taylor's exposition we are invited to open the curtain on the multimedia experience of the throne room in Revelation 4. Merely a glimpse gives us a lot to take in, as we see and hear the multiple splendors and sounds and events, and it prompts us to respond.

Alan Hayes draws from the insights of neuro-psychology to pull us away from our tendency to blanket our perceptions of pain and discomfort and ignore the difficult passages of John's Apocalypse. In "Unsealing the Scroll:

Facing What We Repress," we move past the tendency of our brains to protect us from the realities in the world, and experience anew the reality of war, famine, death, etc., in the seven horses of Revelation 6.

John's Apocalypse is so rich with meaning that it is also a picture of the gospel, as shown to us by Ann Jervis in her meditation on Revelation 7. In "Who is able to stand," the question of who can stand before the judgment of God is answered: We stand not by our own power, but by being washed in the blood of the lamb.

Peter Robinson, in "'Take and Eat': Knowing God in Worship," gives an exposition of Revelation 8–11 that discusses the difficult topic of theodicy—Why does a good God allow people to suffer? His questioning and exploration never answers the question, and in fact, questions the tendency to explain, bringing us finally to worship in the midst of the challenges.

Judy Paulsen offers a pastoral response to Revelation 12 with her exploration of a prominent theme in John's Apocalypse, "Standing Fast in the Meantime." In the midst of the world and its difficulty and suffering, the tendency to decode Revelation is not the appropriate response so much as standing fast in our faith.

In David Kupp's meditation, we shift our perspective to "Reading Babylon from the Margins." We read the judgment of Babylon in Revelation 18 from the perspective of the poor and disenfranchised, and empathize with the call for judgment and justice over those who take advantage of the poor and disenfranchised. Because reading from the margins may not be our true perspective, Kupp also provokes us to ask in what way we are Babylon?

As in a number of these meditations, Murray Henderson also deals with a tough question. "Is God Violent?

Implications for Christians" is his exposition of Revelation 18–19. Here he discusses an aspect of John's Apocalypse that proves difficult for many, the difficulty of God's violence. Here we consider the importance of God's violence while making the distinction between God's part and our part.

Thomas P. Power, in "He Will Come Again to Judge the Living and the Dead," reads Revelation 20 as a depiction of God's sovereignty, justice, judgment, and grace. What does Revelation 20 tell us about these central ideas of Christian theology?

Catherine Sider Hamilton's exposition of Revelation 21–22:5, "The Tree of Life," is almost like the song she begins with, as she lyrically describes the motif of the tree of life, weaving in songs, lamentations, and poems of the tree in the midst of the city of God, Jesus, the tree of life, and the tree upon which Jesus died for us.

In the final meditation, "In the Fullness of Time," Stephen Andrews points out the ways that time is used in Revelation, and how this informs our lives. Appropriately, this final meditation points us to prayer—suggesting that we participate in the fullness of time within our own time by coming before the throne of grace.

These meditations began as a series of sermons at Wycliffe College in the Thursday morning chapel series. The first sermon by Joseph Mangina began with the statement, "Can you hear the liturgy? Can you hear the heavenly worship?" It is my hope and expectation that this little book of meditations will help you to hear and experience the reality of John's Apocalypse, and that, as the text promises, "You will be blessed" (Rev 1:3).

1

An Encounter with the Living One: Revelation and the Healing Invasion of God

JOSEPH MANGINA

THE BOOK OF REVELATION opens with a bang, bombarding us with a flurry of words, visions, and images that disorient and confuse us, and the assault does not relent over the following twenty-two chapters. Revelation does not want to argue or convince us of anything. It is too late for that: "The time is near" (Rev 1:3; 22:10), "Behold, I am coming soon" (Rev 22:7, 12; cf. 22:20). Rather, the book seeks to capture our hearts, renew our love grown cold, strengthen us for resistance to the ungodly powers, and summon us to that patient endurance without which we have no hope of being saved. Like the LORD God himself, the book of Revelation seeks neither our assent nor our approbation, but only our obedience.

What *is* Revelation, anyway? It is, to begin with, an apocalypse, or rather *the* Apocalypse—its name in Greek, and perhaps a better name; "Revelation" (from the Latin *revelatio*) sounds just a bit too intellectual and cognitive. *Apocalypsis* means a disclosure, an uncovering or unsealing of heavenly mysteries—the mysteries of God! Events of this sort are a regular feature of Israel's Scriptures, usually occurring at some critical juncture in the biblical story. Jacob falls asleep and dreams of a ladder reaching to heaven, with the angels of God ascending and descending upon it. He awakens and exclaims, "This is none other than the house of God, and this is the gate of heaven" (Gen 28:17). Centuries later, Ezekiel finds himself among the exiles by the river Chedar, where he receives visions of God, beginning with the divine chariot supported by the *kerubim* and their whirling, many-eyed wheels (Ezek 1). Then, in Mark's account of Jesus' baptism, we are told that Jesus saw "the heavens opened and the Spirit of God descending on him like a dove" (Mark 1:10). Again, in John's gospel, when Nathan expresses astonishment that Jesus saw him under the fig tree, Jesus declares "You will see greater things than these . . . You will see heaven opened, and the angels of God ascending and descending upon the Son of Man" (John 1:51). Notice the important role that angels or angelic beings play in many of these stories. They indicate that something is going on beyond all earthly reckoning; that the world of ordinary experience is not all that there is; that our lives cannot be limited to the grim story of biological determinism and moral nihilism that is our culture's default narrative concerning human nature and destiny. When the heavens open, when God is revealed, earth itself appears in an entirely different light. "Nature" is now shown to be "creation," and when the Creator has dealings with his creatures, anything can happen. This is very good news indeed.

Revelation is not simply "an" apocalypse, however, whether in Scripture itself or in Jewish tradition. It is *the* Apocalypse—*apokalypsis Iesou Christou*, the apocalypse of

Jesus Christ. Does that mean Jesus is the one who does the revealing, or does it mean that Jesus is himself the substance and content of the revelation? Yes. It is both these things. God gives the revelation to Jesus, who gives it to an angel, who delivers it to John, who writes it on a scroll and shares it with the seven churches. Christ is the medium, but he is also the message. He *is* the very word of God itself, as we are told quite explicitly in Revelation 19:13. So here is a piece of counsel: read the Apocalypse as one long exercise in de-familiarization that forces us to re-examine the Jesus we thought we knew:

> When I saw him, I fell at his feet as though dead.
> But he laid his right hand on me, saying, Fear
> not, I am the first and the last, and the living one.
> I died, and behold I am alive forevermore, and
> I have the keys of Death and Hades (Rev 1:17).

Jesus is not only alive, he is *the living one*. He did battle with Death, and Death won, which is to say, Death lost. To be joined to him is to know and experience the very life that God is and that God wills for his creatures. If one had to choose a single theme that runs through the Bible it might well be that of *life*, although often life appears *sub contrario*, under its opposite, the experience of death and judgment. The Apocalypse is one long demonstration of this truth. As we hear the book and let its visions wash over us, we are caught up in the reality of the God of life, named in treble as the One who is, and who was, and who is to come; as Jesus Christ the faithful witness; and as the seven spirits before the divine throne—a liturgical and doxological way of saying the Father, the Son, and the Holy Spirit, who is none other than the LORD God of Israel (Rev 1:4–5). As you read Revelation, never forget that you are reading a Jewish book, although it is a Judaism that (like

Paul's) has been seized by the revelation and authority of Jesus Messiah.

What is Revelation, again? It is not only an apocalypse, but a prophecy, uttered "in the Spirit" (Rev 1:10). The prophet is commissioned to speak the Word of the Lord to the Lord's people in a particular historical moment—usually when the fate of the covenant hangs in the balance. The Lord is faithful to his covenant, but will Israel be faithful? Or in the case of the Apocalypse, will the church be faithful? As usual, the Lord's Word is hard to hear, but it is a Word that we cannot live without, for it is life and health and salvation for us. In his great, difficult book *The Identity of Jesus Christ*,[1] theologian Hans Frei speaks of the Christian as one whose pattern of life "has seemingly suffered an inexplicably wounding and healing invasion"—an invasion by the grace of God. Frei had in mind, I think, primarily the individual experience of grace, but his words are apt on a broader scale. We, the church, are those who live by the wounding and healing invasion of the Word. That is why we cling to the words of this prophecy. It is why the Apocalypse is indispensable.

What is Revelation—one last time? What we call the *book* of Revelation is in fact a letter: "John to the seven churches that are in Asia: Grace to you and peace from the one who is, and who was, and who is to come" (Rev 1:4). That Revelation is a letter might not seem obvious amid all the apocalyptic fireworks, and certainly St. John's epistle is very different from those of St. Paul—although you might want to read Revelation side by side with Romans 8! Still, John the Seer shares his visions with the Christian assemblies in seven cities of Asia Minor. John is joined to his churches in a relation of profound solidarity:

1. Frei, *Identity of Jesus Christ*, 70.

"I, John, your brother who share with you in Jesus the persecution and the kingdom and the patient endurance, was on the island called Patmos because of the word of God and the testimony of Jesus" (John 1:9). It is this solidarity in suffering that lends credibility to John's testimony. The Apocalypse is played out on a historical, political, even cosmic scale, but it is also local and particular—lived out in the daily lives of those baptized into Christ's death and resurrection. The Lord apocalypses himself in Ephesus and Smyrna and Pergamum, in the shadow of empire and the reality of persecution; and he apocalypses himself into our own lives, cities, and homes in these strange, late modern times—a post-Christendom that is perhaps not unlike the pre-Christendom of John and his churches. Strange times, and yet the Lord's time, as the risen Jesus shows himself among us. We are the ones who suffer his wounding and healing invasion. "Blessed is the one who reads aloud the words of the prophecy, and blessed are those who hear and who keep what is written in it; for the time is near" (Rev 1:3). Amen.

Revelation 1

Questions for Further Reflection

1. Read Revelation 1. How is this book an apocalypse? What words and images disclose the heavenly world? Who addresses the readers and what do they say?

2. How is the apocalypse revealing Jesus Christ? How is Jesus described? Is this a different perspective of Jesus from what you know or what is common?

3. The apocalypse is written as a letter to ordinary Christians in their ordinary lives. How are the readers/hearers described? How does this impact your own reading of the text?

4. What does it say about Revelation that its culminating vision is of a city, the "New Jerusalem"? What clues does this give us about God's intentions for humanity?

2

Babylon, the New Jerusalem, and the Cities in Between

TERENCE L. DONALDSON

THE BOOK OF REVELATION is in large measure the story of two great cities and the conflict between them. On one side there is Babylon—"the great city that rules over the kings of the earth" (17:18); "Babylon the great, mother of prostitutes and of earth's abominations, drunk with the blood of the saints" (17:5). On the other side is the New Jerusalem—"the holy city, coming down out of heaven from God, prepared as a bride adorned for her husband" (21:2); Jerusalem, the city by whose light the nations of the earth will walk (21:24), the city in which "death shall be no more" (21:4).

Both of them are linked in essential ways with real, bricks-and-mortar earthly cities. Babylon's earthly manifestation is clearly the city of Rome, the city set on "seven hills" (17:9). This city of Rome/Babylon is at the center of a world-wide empire of subjugation, domination, exploitation, and wealth. The New Jerusalem, of course, is the purified and renewed version of earthly Jerusalem, described elsewhere in Revelation as the "holy city" (11:2) and the "beloved city" (20:9).

But the cities and the conflict between them exist at a more cosmic level as well. The cities are archetypical as well as actual. As with other apocalyptic literature of the period, the conflict experienced by the faithful people of God is just the earthly manifestation of spiritual realities and conflicts taking place at a cosmic or heavenly level. Chapters 6 to 22 of Revelation tell the story of this two-level conflict—a story graphic in its detail and sometimes confusing in its sequence, but a story whose outcome is clear: the final overthrow of Babylon and the appearance of the New Jerusalem, the center of a new, world-wide kingdom of justice, peace, healing, and the joyful presence of God.

John, the prophet who reveals this apocalyptic "tale of two cities," believes that the storm clouds of the coming conflict are already visible, especially in instances of persecution that are being experienced by believers in Jesus. And so, he writes to warn his readers of what is to come and to prepare them to stand firm in face of the ordeal that will soon fall upon them. This brings us to chapters 2 and 3—the focus of this brief meditation.

Babylon and the New Jerusalem are not the only cities in the book of Revelation. John addresses his work to churches in seven additional cities, all located in the Roman province of Asia (western Turkey, in today's geographical terms). Chapters 2 and 3 contain letters addressed to the churches in these cities: Ephesus, Smyrna, Pergamum, Thyatira, Sardis, Philadelphia, and Laodicea. Each of the letters follows a similar pattern: a statement identifying the content of the letter as the words of the risen Jesus, who is then described in terms that echo the vision in chapter 1; a word of praise for positive aspects of the church's faith and witness; a corresponding word of rebuke for ways in which they have fallen short or compromised their loyalties; and finally some words about the future, usually combining warnings of judgment and promises of salvation, with a special promise to "the one who conquers," probably a reference to those who stand firm to the point of martyrdom.

These cities are frequently mentioned in Greco-Roman writings; in addition, there are significant archaeological remains, especially in the case of those that have not been buried under modern cities—specifically Ephesus, Pergamum, Sardis, and Laodicea. Thus we can know quite a bit about them and about what daily life might have been like in the first century. All of them came under Roman rule in the second century before Christ, and they enjoyed a fairly peaceful and prosperous existence in the centuries that followed. I have had a couple of opportunities over the years to tramp through these archaeological sites. Spending time in these sites, one readily begins to imagine the everyday life of the people who once lived there, especially as one walks along the ancient streets and sees things that would have been part of their daily existence: colonnaded walkways alongside the main streets; shops lining the streets or opening onto the colonnades; theatres, stadiums, and meeting halls; public baths and gymnasiums; aqueducts, public fountains, and other water supply installations; luxury houses and humble apartment blocks; and all of this in a very pleasant climate. I probably wasn't the only one who found myself thinking that if I had been born in the first century, this would have been a pretty good place to live.

And so, reading these letters from our vantage point and with a little bit of knowledge about the world of the first readers, we cannot help but wonder—or at least I can't help wondering—how the letters would have struck them, as they went about their daily lives in one or other of these cities. Now I certainly don't want to paint an unrealistically rosy picture of the situation facing urban Christians in the late first century. Those who benefited most from the peace and prosperity enjoyed by these cities were the ones at the top of the social scale; for those farther down, life would have been more of a struggle. Further, Christians faced a lot of negative social pressure—dislike, hostility, discrimination, persecution, occasionally going as far as martyrdom. And a lot of this was at least tolerated and sometimes carried out by civic and imperial authorities. Still, the lines that John was drawing between Babylon and the New Jerusalem were stark, clear, and uncompromising, whereas many aspects of their own daily lives would have seemed to them, no doubt, to occupy a much more ambiguous area in between the two.

Further, John devotes much of his letters to warnings about traits and behavior that he fears will put some of them on the wrong side of the line. Again, I don't want to downplay the significance of these things—accepting false teachers, eating meat that had been sacrificed to polytheistic gods in local temples, complacency in Christian devotion and discipleship, sexual immorality (though the term is probably metaphorical for the worship of other gods). Still, to pick up on just one of these: John's attitude towards meat sacrificed to idols is quite extreme, especially when compared to the more nuanced position that Paul puts forward in his Corinthian letters. Again, one cannot help thinking that Christian existence in these seven cities was characterized by much more ambiguity than John's sharp line of division seems to permit.

In addition, although John says that he is writing about things that will "soon take place" (1:1) and says to the believers in Philadelphia that Jesus "is coming soon" (3:11), we are well aware that we, just like the original readers of Revelation, are still living on this side of the apocalypse. We, like them, also find ourselves living in the ambiguous space between Babylon and the New Jerusalem.

So, my question about the original readers is also our own question. As we read John's letters to the churches in these seven cities, sitting here in our own cities, what are we to make of them, and of the larger revelation for which they serve as an introduction?

I mentioned a moment ago that Revelation belongs to a body of literature that juxtaposes events taking place on two interconnected levels—the earthly and the cosmic (or heavenly). A similar kind of juxtaposition happens in the temporal dimension as well. One of the features of prophetic and apocalyptic literature is that it juxtaposes two crisis moments—a perceived situation of crisis facing the people of God in the present, and the larger, more ultimate crisis that will come in the future. This, I suggest, might help us as we read the book of Revelation. John places the crisis that he sees emerging in the present against the background of the crisis that will precede Christ's coming in the future—a crisis that will pit the forces of evil against the purposes of God, and that will bring this age to an end and culminate in the establishment of God's kingdom.

The purpose of this prophetic juxtaposition, however, is not to provide us with a speculative timetable of future events, despite the attempts of zealous and zany television evangelists to tell us otherwise. Rather, its purpose has to do more with the present than the future. In order to make sense of our present situation in all its ambiguity and perplexity, we need to see our own circumstances against the background of the final ultimate crisis, where extraneous issues will be stripped away and fundamental issues will stand out in all their clarity. In order to know how to shape our lives as Christian persons and communities now, we need to start with what we have been given to know about the end and then work backwards to the present.

What have we been given to know about the end? Well, the answers to this question will weave their way through the remainder of this preaching series. But perhaps the most important thing is this: The ultimate question that will face us is whether our allegiance will be given to Christ and the God whom he reveals—whether, when the lines are clearly drawn, we will be found on the side of the line that marks out the kingdom of God and of his Christ. This is not to say that nothing else matters; rather, in the end, when the mists are lifted and reality is laid fully open to view, it will be clearly seen how all that matters is grounded in and bounded by Christ himself. This is the future within which we need to place our present existence; this is the future on which we need to fix our eyes as we continue to live in that ambiguous space between Babylon and the New Jerusalem.

Revelation 2–3

Questions for Further Reflection

1. Read through Revelation 2–3, noticing the opening section of each letter ("These are the words of . . . "). Look at the way in which Christ is described in each and compare each description with the ways in which

Christ is described and referred to in chapter 1. What points of connection do you observe?

2. Thinking of a church or congregation with which you identify closely (your current congregation or one in your past), compare it in its strengths and weaknesses with the seven churches described in chapters 2 and 3. Can you identify one or two for which the resemblance is particularly strong or revealing? What aspects (positive or negative) of your own church are not reflected in these seven descriptions at all?

3. What can we learn from these chapters about Christian existence in our own day, as we experience the ambiguities of life in the space between Babylon and the New Jerusalem?

3

"Come up Here": A Glimpse of Heaven

MARION TAYLOR

WITH REVELATION CHAPTER 4, we move from the letters that censure the seven churches (Rev 3–4) to an awe-inspiring heavenly scene. In her little known commentary on the book of Revelation, renowned nineteenth-century poet and commentator Christina Rossetti speaks about the significance of the change in scene with the prayer, "O Lord, Thou hast reproved the Churches, and we have heard Thy reproof. Turn us, we beseech Thee, and teach us by Thy most Holy Spirit the meaning of Thy sacred words."[2] May this be our prayer also, as we meditate on this remarkable heavenly scene. May the Lord teach us by his most Holy Spirit the meaning of his sacred words.

Chapter 4 begins with John looking and seeing an open door in heaven. He hears a voice like a trumpet inviting him to "Come up here . . . where I will show you what must take place after this." We too are invited to come up

2. Rossetti, *Face of the Deep*, 149. Rossetti was one of thirty women who wrote commentaries on the book of Revelation according to Kachur, "Getting the Last Word," 1–72.

and look with John, and yet like Isaiah we are conscious of our utter unworthiness to view the throne room of God where the seraphim call to one another, "Holy, holy, holy is the Lord of Hosts, the whole earth is full of his glory" (Isa 6:3). In Isaiah, the prophet responds to seeing the king, the Lord of Lords, "Woe is me! I am lost, for I am a man of unclean lips, and I live among a people of unclean lips!" (Isa 6:5).

As we are invited in through the open door to gaze and experience the glorious scene revealed to John, we too should be conscious of our unworthiness. And yet as the very humble Rossetti recognized, we need to enter because "to gaze in whatever ignorance on what God reveals, is so far to do His will."[3] And so, in what Joseph Mangina calls "truly a liminal passage," we cross "a threshold from what can be humanly experienced and imagined to what lies beyond our ken."[4]

What John in the spirit sees inside the open door is a throne. Thrones are very important to John; he mentions "throne" forty-seven times in the book of Revelation—it occurs elsewhere in the New Testament only fifteen times. The throne John sees is not an earthly throne, but rather the throne of God. John is circumspect in what he describes. He uses images and metaphors that arouse our senses of sight and sound. And yet, as artists, musicians, commentators, and really all careful readers recognize, the scene he describes is imprecise and leaves much to the sanctified imagination.

The one seated on the throne is described in terms of the brilliance of precious and semi-precious stones. The stone John calls jasper may be the mineral we call

3. Rossetti, *Face of the Deep*, 146.

4. Mangina, *Revelation*, 74.

jasper—a stone that is opaque and comes in many colors. This jasper is, however, more likely the clear and dazzling stone named jasper found in Revelation 21:11, where the holy city Jerusalem is described as having "a radiance like a very rare jewel, like jasper, clear as crystal" (Rev 21:11). The radiant Holy One on the throne is also likened to the fiery red stone carnelian.

This same glorious throne is encircled with a rainbow that is unlike any rainbow we have ever seen. It does not contain the prism of colors we associate with rainbows— red, orange, yellow, green, blue, indigo, and violet. Rather, this heavenly rainbow is emerald green. It recalls the rainbow Ezekiel used to describe the splendor that surrounded his heavenly vision of the glory of the Lord (Ezek 1:28). It also reminds us of the eternal covenant of peace God made with Noah (Gen 9:16). If the color of this unique emerald green rainbow has significance, as some suggest, it may point to God's mercy (Ps 52:8) or symbolize hope—the kind of hope that the greenery of spring offers—or perhaps the refreshing calm that green brings to the eye.

Also around the Lord's throne are twenty-four thrones for the twenty-four crowned elders wearing white robes. Again, there is much debate about these twenty-four elders. Some think that they are angelic beings who represent the faithful. Others suggest that they signify the twelve tribes of Israel and the twelve apostles. Still others think that the elders recall the twenty-four orders of priests in 1 Chronicles 24:4–19. And yet others draw on numerology, astronomy, or astrology to help identify the twenty-four elders. But more important than the identity of the twenty-four elders is their function, which Mounce describes as "both royal and sacerdotal, and may be judicial as well (cf.

20:4). Their white garments speak of holiness, and their golden crowns of royalty."[5]

This heavenly scene is a feast not only for the eyes but also for the ears as we see the flashes of lighting coming from the throne, and hear rumblings and peals of thunder that remind us of terrifying manifestations of God's power and glory at Sinai that left God's people trembling in fear (Exod 19:16). In front of the throne are seven flaming torches that represent the person of God the Holy Spirit (cf. Rev 1:4). Some also associate the seven flaming torches with the seven spirits of the Lord described by Isaiah: "The spirit of the Lord shall rest on him, the spirit of wisdom and understanding, the spirit of counsel and might, the spirit of knowledge and the fear of the Lord" (Isa 11:2). This vision of the seven flaming torches inspired Rossetti to write "A Prayer to the Holy Spirit," which draws on the rich bank of metaphors and similes found in scripture:

O God the Holy Ghost

Who art light unto thine elect

Evermore enlighten us.

Thou who art fire of love

Evermore enkindle us.

Thou who art Lord and Giver of Life,

Evermore live in us.

Thou who bestowest sevenfold grace,

Evermore replenish us.

As the wind is thy symbol,

So forward our goings.

As the dove, so launch us heavenwards.

As water, so purify our spirits.

As a cloud, so abate our temptations.

5. Mounce, *Book of Revelation*, 136.

As dew, so revive our languor.

As fire, so purge our dross.[6]

As we move further away from the throne, John shows us something that is not a sea but something like a sea of glass that is likened to crystal. Like many other things in this chapter, the full significance of the reflective sea in front of the throne is not known.

The tour of God's throne room continues as we are shown four winged, living creatures whose all-seeing eyes are described as being both "in front and behind" and "all around and inside" (Rev 4:6, 8). The creatures are very like the cherubim shown to Ezekiel, but they have six wings like the seraphs in Isaiah's vision. And unlike each of Ezekiel's four-faced creatures, these heavenly creatures have unique faces: one has a man's face, one a lion's face, one the face of an ox, and one the face of a flying eagle. Commenting on the significance of the four faces of Ezekiel's creatures and their place in the divine vision, one early rabbi explained: "Man is exalted among creatures, the eagle among birds, the ox among domestic animals, the lion among wild beasts; all of them have received dominion . . . . Yet they are stationed below the chariot of the Holy One."[7] So too Swete probes the significance of the faces of the creatures John sees and suggests that "The four forms represent whatever is noblest, strongest, wisest and swiftest in animate Nature." He also notes that all Nature is represented before the throne—birds, domestic animals, wild animals, and humans—"taking its part in the fulfilment of the Divine Will, and the worship of the divine Majesty."[8]

---

6. Rossetti, *Face of the Deep*, 155.

7. *Midrash Shemoth* R.23, quoted in Mangina, *Revelation*, 78.

8. Henry B. Swete as cited in Morris, *Revelation of St. John*, 91.

The magnificent living creatures before God's throne sing a variation of the song the seraphim sang in Isaiah 6: "Holy, Holy, Holy is the Lord Almighty, the whole earth is full of his glory." The second line of the living creatures' heavenly song is different. Its focus is not God's glorifying presence on the earth alone, but rather the Lord Almighty, who is described in terms of time and eternity—"Holy, Holy, Holy, the Lord God Almighty who was and is and is to come" (Rev 4:8).

The worship the living creatures offer continues day and night—they sing while we are awake and they sing while we sleep, "their endless worship being an endless contentment, their labour a labour of love, their exploration of unfathomable mysteries as it were a skylark's ever-ascending fight; yet even at the same moment, as his sustained exaltation at his zenith on poised wings . . . Their worship is due exercise of their gifts; the exercise of their gifts is worship."[9]

The twenty-four elders respond to the worship of the living creatures by falling adoringly before the eternal one seated on the throne. And as an act of their selfless devotion and love, they give back the crowns to the one who gave them and proclaim:

You are worthy, our lord and God,

To receive glory and honor and power.

For you created all things,

And by your will they existed and were created (Rev 4:11).

The elders' declaration not only proclaims the holiness of God, it also proclaims that God is worthy of glory, honor, and power.

In their worship, these living creatures and elders have much to teach us. Their only object of contemplation

9. Rossetti, *Face of the Deep*, 159.

is the omnipotent God Almighty. Rossetti, who was very conscious of her place in a world that privileged men and discouraged women from doing theology and biblical interpretation, writes, "That same School of Cherubim [and Elders] is open to men." Then, boldly claiming the equality men and women have before God in Christ, she says that this same school "is open to me. True knowledge adores, gives thanks, loves and ever follows on to know the love of Christ, which passeth knowledge."[10]

This focus on God alone reminds us that there is no room for worship of another. "You shall have no other Gods before me." And yet so easily we fall into sin. Citing as evidence a long list of stories in Scripture, Calvin called the human mind "a perpetual forge" or "factory of idols." And it is at this point that we are taken back to the invitation to witness with John what was on the other side of the open door of heaven. We are reminded again of our privilege—as unworthy creatures prone to idolatry—to join in the heavenly chorus and proclaim the holiness of the Lord God the Almighty, who was and is and is to come. And before this same almighty God, today we proclaim God's worthiness to receive glory and honor and power. Amen.

Revelation 4

Questions for Further Reflection

1. Read Revelation 4, observing the sights and sounds. Try to imagine what you would see, hear, and feel if you were able to have this glimpse of heaven. If you can, try to write out your own response.

10. Ibid., 161.

2. Meditate upon the physical and verbal responses of the elders in Revelation 4 and compare the responses of the prophet Isaiah in Isaiah 6, of Ezekiel in Ezekiel 1, and the prayers of Christina Rossetti quoted in this chapter.

4

Unsealing the Scroll: Facing What We Repress

ALAN L. HAYES

THE REVELATION TO ST. John comes to the Church as Scripture. We don't read it as just an interesting ancient text; it comes to us with authority. It's *revelation*. It reveals how things really are, and will be, and have been. Other texts create their own realities and describe worlds that are very engaging, but when we put down a novel like *Pride and Prejudice*, we leave our imaginative time in Pemberley and return to our ordinary world where we look out the window and see a familiar scene and check the weather. When we put down the Revelation to St. John, we're not supposed to say, "Well, now back to the real world!" We're supposed to say, "Somewhere in there, in or behind those stories of four horsemen of the apocalypse riding across the earth, is a revelation of things that are more real than my familiar, common-sense experience of reality!" In the end, what do we trust? Do we trust our experience of reality? Or do we trust what Scripture reveals about reality?

Before we examine Revelation 6, it's worthwhile to recognize that the reality we experience is highly

constructed. This is true simply physiologically and neu-
rologically. About a third of our brain cortex is devoted to
seeing. We open our eyes and about 140 million neurons
go to work to make sense of it all. That's a lot of neurons,
and they're doing a lot more than receiving optical images.
What they're mainly doing is making sense of what we're
looking at.[11] One way we know that what we're seeing may
not be real is by experiencing optical illusions. Some of us
may have experienced optical illusions where we *look at* a
totally weird, lopsided, slanted room but what we *see* is a
lovely rectangular room, because our brains make things
look like what our brains think they ought to look like.[12]
Or, again, we may think that we inhabit a space where we
can move in any direction in a time which only moves
forward, but one of Einstein's discoveries that has been
frequently verified on an astronomical level over the past
century is that space and time are actually one continuum;
and, as Einstein said, past, present, and future are a stubbornly persistent illusion.[13] What our brains do for us is
create a usable interface with reality. It's like our smartphones that give us screens with icons to work with because the actual realities of smartphones with their circuits
and diodes and chips are beyond our comprehension and
control. What our brains do is show us a usable interface
like a smartphone screen, and the interface makes sure
that we don't have to deal with things that are inconsistent
with our assumptions, or that don't make sense, or that we

11. See the "Ted Talk" by Donald Hoffman, "Do We See Reality
As It Is?"

12. Like the one at the Ontario Science Centre in Toronto.

13. See for instance Hawking, *Stubbornly Persistent Illusion*, back
cover. Admittedly, Einsteinian views of time do not cohere with
quantum theories; but quantum physics also presents reality as very
different from our ordinary experience.

just shouldn't have to worry about. As a result, our personalities are shaped by filtered perceptions, by persistent irrational beliefs, and by false memories.

Our brains invent things and they filter out things. Filtering out extraneous data is generally a good thing. I have a daughter whose brain doesn't always do a very good job of excluding irrelevant and miscellaneous data, and that's considered a problem—called borderline attention deficit. When she had to write examinations in school, she paid as much attention to a ticking clock or a crinkling kleenex or a spider spinning a web as to the test in front of her, because her brain didn't let her ignore those things as it was supposed to. While that was a problem for tests, it's great for driving a car because she sees everything that's going on around her, can anticipate potential accidents, and never loses her way.

My other daughter and I watched an old episode of (dare I say it?) "Buffy the Vampire Slayer," where Buffy is infected by a demon, becomes telepathic, and suddenly can hear and feel all the hurt and unhappiness and anxiety of everyone around her, and it just about drives her crazy.[14] If you actually had to be in touch with all the terrible realities of human experience, you'd go crazy. If right now we had to have an I–Thou relationship with everyone in this room and enter into their worries and disappointments and longings, how long would we last? So our brains protect us from noticing too many other people and from entering sympathetically into their realities.

All that to say that the book of Revelation is dangerous. It functions as something like an invitation to insanity because it puts us in touch with all of that pain and it gives us the revelation of what actually is, once we've removed

14. "Earshot," series 3, episode 18.

all those beneficial self-deceptions. It shows us the world when our ego drops out of the equation.[15] It opens up a scroll that we try to keep rolled up so that we won't be undone and overwhelmed by the truth of things.

So, foreboding comes over us as the Lamb, who is Jesus Christ, undoes the seals on the scroll that have been put there for our protection. And as the Lamb breaks the seals, one by one, reality begins to confront us.

The Lamb breaks a seal, and we see a rider on a fiery red horse, who receives a sword and has the power to take peace from the earth (Rev 6:3–4). Here is the reality of war. Don't let anyone tell you that the book of Revelation gives predictions of things that will happen at some future date. The book of Revelation doesn't predict; it reveals. We don't even have to wait for war. It's happening now, even if it may not touch us. Within the past year there have been tens of thousands of deaths from war in Afghanistan, Iraq, Syria, Mexico (the drug war), Myanmar, Libya, Somalia, South Sudan, Central African Republic, Yemen, Darfur, Kashmir, Ukraine, Congo, Peru, and dozens of other places.[16] Almost half a million people have died in Syria alone over the past six years. The United States, Canada, and most European countries are involved in wars. In fact, if you count the countries of the world that are *not* involved in wars, you can't get past about a dozen. They include Iceland, New Zealand, Mauritius, Switzerland, and Japan.[17] Does our experience of the world include the terrible realities of war? For some of us, no doubt, the answer is yes, if war has

15. Frye, "Revelation: After the Ego Disappears."

16. "List of Ongoing Conflicts," Wikipedia.

17. The Global Peace Index is published annually by the Institute for Economics and Peace, a think tank with offices in Sydney, New York, and The Hague, https://reliefweb.int/report/world/global-peace-index-2017.

touched our lives; but otherwise, St. John the Divine shows us the fiery red horse.

The Lamb breaks another seal, and we see a rider on a black horse weighing out bits of wheat and selling them at outrageous prices, and this shows us the face of famine (Rev 6:5–6). In the modern conventions of international aid, famine defines a specific situation verified by three criteria, and by that definition twenty million people are experiencing famine right now in Somalia, South Sudan, Nigeria, and Yemen. According to the United Nations, this sweeping band of famine is the worst global emergency since World War II.[18] Another fifty million people in the world need emergency food. Do we see the black horse? If we eat well, we may not see it. Or maybe some of us have experienced the ravages of famine first-hand. But in case we've filtered out from our experience of reality the sufferings of the world's hungry, St. John the Divine shows us the black horse.

The Lamb breaks another seal, and we see a rider on a pale green horse, and the text names this rider; his name is Death (Rev 6:7–8). The Anglican Prayer Book states that in the midst of life, we are in death. And that's true. The fact is, at each second, we ourselves and everyone we love are at risk of death. Usually, we repress the dread of death, but not always. If you had been in Hawaii on January 13, 2018, you would have received a message, mistakenly sent from the government, warning you of imminent obliteration.[19] But we could hardly live out a day if we continually had to bear the burden of that knowledge, and we certainly would find it hard to make a lot of long-range plans or concen-

18. Associated Press, "U.N. Says World Faces Largest Humanitarian Crisis Since World War II," published in various outlets including *The Wall Street Journal*, March 11, 2017.

19. "Hawaii Panics," *New York Times*, January 13, 2018.

trate on small tasks. So, usually, though not always, we act on the assumption that life will go on indefinitely. But the fact is, a hundred people in the world die every minute.[20] In the time you have been reading this, a thousand more people are dead. They die of heart disease, stroke, lower respiratory infections, cancer, diabetes, dementia, accidents, murder, suicides. The people who die are people that their families and friends love. Many are children. Many suffer. And it would drive us crazy to have to think about that all the time, so mostly we don't, though maybe some of us do, if we've recently been touched by death. But in case we're filtering out from our experience of reality the certainty of death and the possibility of sudden death, St. John the Divine shows us the pale green horse.

The Lamb opens another seal, and St. John sees the souls of those who are persecuted for the word of God, and they are all under the altar of God (Rev 6:9–11). Open Doors, an organization that verifies the persecution of Christians, calculates that over 1,200 Christians died last year as a result of religious persecution.[21] On Palm Sunday last year, two Coptic churches in Egypt were bombed by terrorists, and forty-four Christians died. So many Christians have been killed by ISIS that the U.S. Department of State has described those murders as part of a genocide. And the number 1,200 is a highly conservative one. That's the number of individuals whose deaths have been independently verified and specifically factually attributed to persecution. It therefore doesn't even include suspected Christian deaths in North Korea or in war zones such as Syria and Iraq. If we included whole populations that

20. The Ecology Global Network, "World Birth and Death Rates."

21. Open Doors is a non-denominational Christian mission which monitors persecution and delivers bibles. The website of its Canadian branch is at http://www.opendoorsca.org/.

suffer persecution en masse partly because they identify as Christian, there would be thousands more. Do we recognize the mortal dangers of being a Christian? Probably not so much in Canada, though maybe some in this room have been touched by religious persecution. So, in case we've filtered out from our experience of reality the price that many people in the world have to pay for loving Jesus Christ, St. John the Divine shows us the souls under God's altar.

The Lamb opens another seal on the scroll, and all the populations of the world, slave and free, the mighty and rich and everyone else, try to hide from the wrath of God (Rev 6:12–17). Many of us may not worry a great deal about the wrath of God because we'd rather not acknowledge that we deserve God's anger. Yes, we may join regularly in reading out a general confession, but since it's a general confession it just tells us that we're "no worse than anyone else." And when it comes down to the particulars of practice, the sins we're willing to acknowledge when they do happen may tend to be very small sins, like letting slip a cuss word or procrastinating. If we do something that really hurts someone else cruelly, if we're like most people, we find ways to justify it.[22] We say, "it wasn't really my fault," or "I didn't have a choice," or "other people are just too sensitive," or "they deserved it," or "it wasn't really that big a deal." The bigger the sin, the more we excuse ourselves, because part of what allows most of us to survive from day to day is the belief that really, all things considered, I'm a pretty good person. But when the Lamb opens the sixth seal, we discover the reality that we've tried to leech out of our reading of Scripture and out of our understanding

22. See Lerner, "Why That Person Who Hurt You Will Never Apologize."

of the gospel and out of our conception of ourselves, the reality that we deserve God's righteous anger.

But there's one more reality. It's actually the first one in Revelation 6, but I have left it for last. The first horseman of the Apocalypse rides on a white charger and wears a crown and goes out to conquer (Rev 6:1–2). There is much dispute as to who this is, but St. Irenaeus in the second century said this is Christ himself.[23] Others say that it's the Holy Spirit, since Christ has ascended. In either case, God has gone out ahead of war and famine and death and persecution and fear of the wrath of God, and the Spirit of Christ has spread the gospel all over the face of the earth. Christ has won the victory; he has died, once for all, for the salvation of the world. Perhaps strangely, even as Christians, we don't generally allow ourselves to see God personally at work among us. We may even say that Christ has no hands to bless but ours; no eyes to see compassionately but ours; no feet to walk to give help to others but ours;[24] and pretty soon we think that Christ depends on us. But no, it's we who depend on Christ, who has conquered and who wears the crown. And, if St. Irenaeus' interpretation is right, St. John sees the conqueror riding to victory ahead of us.

Christ loves us and is merciful, and so I'm sure Christ recognizes that we need our illusions just to survive the day. But he also gives us this revelation of how things really

23. *Adv. Haer.* IV.20.11. Irenaeus appears to identify the white horse of Revelation 6 with the white horse of Revelation 19. This interpretation has been called the "traditional" one: Considine, "Rider on the White Horse," 406–22.

24. I'm paraphrasing a prayer attributed to Teresa of Avila; it's quoted frequently on the Internet and in sermons. The Institute of Carmelite Studies reportedly affirms that these words don't appear in any authenticated writing by Teresa; see Chonak, "No, Saint Whoever Did Not Actually Say That."

are—a world where pain and terrors are all around us, but at the same time a world where Christ has ridden ahead in victory. The extent of the world's pain and worry is beyond our capacity to take in, and yet God goes ahead, victorious over everything that threatens us, assuring us that love wears the crown. For that assurance, thanks be to God!

Revelation 6

Questions for Further Reflection

1. This meditation sees Revelation as a picture of present reality; others take it to be a prophecy of things to come, either political or cosmic; and still others take it to be a set of symbols of the Roman Empire. What do you think?

2. Do you agree that our experience of reality is highly constructed, and that we see what we want to see and repress what creates problems for us? Can you think of examples in your own life that would confirm or challenge this view of things?

3. Do you agree that in our understanding of the world, most of us, most of the time, tend to marginalize war, famine, death, and persecution, unless we've had a personal experience of it?

4. The theology of God's anger had a prominent place in much of Christian history, but here's what the late R. P. C. Hanson, an Anglican church historian and Church of Ireland bishop, said about it: "Most preachers and most composers of prayers today treat the biblical doctrine of the wrath of God very much as the Victorians treated sex. It is there, but it must

never be alluded to because it is in an undefined way shameful . . . . God is love; therefore we must not associate him with wrath." Perhaps the idea of God's anger is more common today in some evangelical churches than in mainline denominations. Have you found it a helpful idea, a damaging idea, a disturbing idea, a Biblical idea, an un-Biblical idea, an irrelevant idea, or something else?

5

Who Is Able to Stand?

Ann Jervis

Revelation 7 answers the question at the close of the preceding chapter, "Who is able to stand?" (Rev 6:17). Chapter 6 describes the Lamb opening six of seven seals. When he opens these seals, terrifying events are unleashed which threaten the earth and its inhabitants. These events signal the Lamb's judgement on sin. By the time the sixth seal is opened near the end of chapter 6, the kings of the earth and the great and rich and powerful—the purveyors of sin—are hiding in caves, calling out to the mountains and rocks, "Fall on us and hide us from the face of the one seated on the throne and from the wrath of the Lamb; for the great day of their wrath has come, and who is able to stand?" (Rev 6:16–17).

Chapter 7 tells us who *is* able to stand. The chapter opens with John saying that after this, he saw four angels standing at the four corners of the earth, holding back the earth's four winds, and an angel ascending from the rising of the sun shouting with a great voice: "Do not damage the earth or the sea or the trees until we have marked the slaves of our God with a seal on their foreheads" (Rev 7:1–3).

In chapter 7, we are given a breather from the horrors of judgement on sin. We are taken to another place—to a place where people are not cowering in caves. In chapter 7, John describes two groups of people who are in vastly different circumstances in relation to divine wrath from the great ones cowering in the caves. First, John hears about a group of people that is protected from the wrath of God and the Lamb by being sealed—as a slave is sealed—tattooed on their foreheads. These protected people are identified as belonging to God. By belonging to God it is guaranteed that they will withstand the coming wrath. These people are from every tribe of the Israelites.

Many interpreters of this passage—going back to Origen—think that John is here identifying the church on earth with Israel. And I think this is right, although I don't think that this carries with it the later idea of supercessionism—the church as an entity distinct from Israel and replacing Israel in God's purposes. For John, God works only in and through Israel. The 144,000 protected ones from the tribes of Israel are not the church replacing Israel, they are Israel. As God has always done, God protects the faithful from God's people.

What John hears about the 144,000 answers the terrified question from the rich and powerful of the earth: those who are able to stand are the ones God marks as God's own from among God's people.

We will meet these 144,000 again. In chapter 14, John doesn't just hear about the 144,000—he sees them. He sees them on Mount Zion standing with the Lamb. Now they have the name of the Lamb and the Father's name written on their foreheads. And they are singing a new song before the throne of God—a song that only they could learn. The

144,000 have now been, as John writes, "ransomed" from the earth (Rev 14:3).

Back to chapter 7, where John sees a second group of people—a group that is comprised of Jews along with people from every nation, people, and language. And, unlike the first group, it is so numerous that, as John writes, "no one could count" their number (Rev 7:9). These people are standing before the throne and the Lamb. They are robed in white with palm branches in their hands, crying with a single great voice, "Salvation belongs to our God who is seated on the throne, and to the Lamb!" (Rev 7:10).

We find out that these worshippers of God and the Lamb have come through what is ahead for the 144,000—the great ordeal, the great tribulation. The life of those who have come through the great ordeal and are now standing around God and the Lamb is free from pain and sorrow; they live now standing and worshipping—waving palm branches, symbols of joy and victory—in front of God and the Lamb to whom alone salvation belongs.

Throughout Revelation, John gives us several vivid visions of worship in heaven. The vision from chapter 7 is one of his most beautiful and vigorous and potent, perhaps because it is a direct answer to the question of the cowering powerful, "Who is able to stand?" The answer is: these innumerable people from every nation, tribe, people, and language. These people who have come through the great tribulation and who have washed their robes and made them white in the blood of the Lamb—these people can stand.

These people can stand because, unlike the great ones of the earth, they are not the objects of divine wrath; no, these people have put their hands in the Lamb's blood—the Lamb's blood that was also their blood. These people whose death, as the commentator Eugene Boring puts it, "became one with the Lamb's death"[25]—these are the people who are standing. They are standing, having made it through the great ordeal by sharing in the Lamb's death. The blood of the martyrs is also the Lamb's blood and the Lamb's blood is also the martyrs' blood. John puts it this way in chapter 12—"they have conquered [the great dragon] by the blood of the Lamb and by the word of their testimony, for they loved not their lives even unto death" (Rev 12:11).

To the powerful people quaking in the caves, God and the Lamb are full of wrath. But the faithful martyrs adore God and the Lamb—the martyrs know that salvation belongs only to the one on the throne and the Lamb at the center of that throne. The ordeal that the faithful martyrs have come through has not made them bitter, it has made them grateful. They are eternally and profoundly grateful that they can stand in the presence of God and the Lamb. They are eternally and profoundly grateful that they see that the Lamb is at the center of the throne—at the center of God's being is the Lamb's sacrifice.

The ordeal they have come through has opened these martyrs to the wondrous pain that is at the heart of God— God's astonishing sacrificial love—a love of immeasurable cost to God and the Lamb. So the martyrs' greatest joy is to stand and worship God and the Lamb, day and night. They know that God's throne, unlike the thrones of the great ones of the earth, does not demand blood. God's throne gives blood—the blood of the Lamb, the life blood of God. Salvation belongs only to God and the Lamb.

Before heading into chapter 8, in which we will witness the opening of the seventh and most terrifying seal, chapter 7 is a reprieve. It offers comfort—assurance of

25. Boring, *Revelation*, 131.

salvation. For John's original context, where testifying to faith in God and the Lamb was life-threatening, John's vision of the protected 144,000 and the saved martyrs in heaven offered encouragement to keep the faith. John puts it this way in chapter 14: "here is a call for the endurance of the saints, those who keep the commandments of God and the faith of Jesus" (Rev 14:12).

As Scripture, John's vision is also a call to us, a call that is both a reassuring encouragement to keep the faith and a sober and serious word to the faithful. The serious word is that deliverance from the wrath of God and the Lamb is not in our power—even if we live faithful and good lives, even if we lay down our lives for God. Paul's words come to mind: "though I give my body to be burned" (1 Cor 13:3).

It is only if God marks us as God's own, and only if we mix our blood with the Lamb's blood that we are saved from God's anger against sin. Life with God is God's to offer, not ours to earn. "Salvation belongs to our God who sits on the throne and to the Lamb!" (Rev 7:10). The joy of the worshippers in white robes is the joy of having given their lives entirely into God's hands. Even their deaths are not *for* God, but *with* God. For it is the Lamb's blood—not theirs alone—which allows them to stand and worship.

John presents the hard truth of our entire dependence on God wrapped in glorious and profoundly reassuring light. We who hear it are assured that we too are saved. Because we witness John's privileged information about God's protective sealing, and because we follow John to God's throne, we know that the worshippers around that throne are our people. These people are us, and God and the Lamb are our saviors, too. We, too, will stand. For, through John, the wonder of who God is has been revealed to us; he is the one who saves, the one who stoops to wipe away every tear, who gives food and water; he is the one at whose center is the Lamb.

Our task, as was that of the faithful in John's time, is to endure and keep the faith in word and in deed. To be assured and to act from the knowledge that God, and the Lamb at God's heart, are stronger than every ruler and power and the evils of sin that reign inside and outside of us. And to keep our faith with profound humility—knowing that our performance in word and deed is not what saves us, but that we will stand because salvation belongs to God and to the Lamb.

Revelation 7

Questions for Further Reflection

1. What do you imagine "the great ordeal" to be?

2. What is the difference between a theology that allows for suicide bombings and one that encourages martyrdom, as we find such in Revelation?

3. What do you think being washed in the Lamb's blood means?

6

"Take and Eat": Knowing God in Worship

PETER ROBINSON

THIS PAST WEEK, A good friend was diagnosed with late-stage cancer. So now we pray. We pray for God's goodness and grace and healing while we also struggle, asking where is God in the midst of this and particularly in our friend's pain? In the face of pain and suffering, it is inevitable that we should raise questions of theodicy—why do bad things happen to good people, and how are we to understand God's judgement of human sinfulness? While it may seem unwise to raise these kinds of questions at the beginning of a short meditation on the apocalyptic imagery of the book of Revelation, the book itself turns our attention to these issues.

There aren't easy answers to the question of judgment—we can't side with the Pat Robertsons of this world and confidently label various events or natural disasters as *the* judgment of God. But neither is it very satisfying to side with the enlightened skeptics and quickly erase any references to judgment. The book of Revelation is full of potent images of the judgement of God, including chapters

8 and 9, where we read of the trumpet plagues: one after another in progressive intensity they pile up, until with the sixth trumpet, one-third of humankind has been killed. And still, those who survive do not repent or give up the worship of false idols (Rev 9:20–21).

Revelation chapter 10 breaks into the midst of the seven trumpet plagues, just as chapter 7 broke into the midst of the seven seals. It opens with an astonishing image: a glorious angel, strong and mighty. Descending from heaven, this towering angel stands with one foot on the sea and one foot on the land, proclaiming authority over all things. Some have speculated that this angel might be Christ himself.[26] He is robed in cloud like the Son of Man in Daniel 7:13; the rainbow over his head recalls Revelation 4:3: "The one who sat there had the appearance of jasper and carnelian. A rainbow, resembling an emerald, encircled the throne."[27] The angel's legs—pillars or columns of fire—remind the reader of the exodus, where God led the people with a pillar of cloud by day and a pillar of fire by night (Exod 13:21). The angel's great shout resonates with Jeremiah 25:30 or Amos 1:2 or Hosea 11:10, where the Lord roars like a lion. It also echoes passages like Psalm 29 as it speaks of the voice of God's authority: "The voice of the Lord is over the waters; the God of glory thunders . . . The voice of the Lord is powerful; the voice of the Lord is full of majesty" (Ps 29:3, 4). The glory of the Lord is present in this angel.

Yet, as important as this angel is, he is not identified directly with Christ but as one who points toward Christ. Standing on both sea and land, he raises his right hand

---

26. "In ver. 1, a mighty angel (probably the Angel of the covenant, the Lord Jesus Christ)." Simeon, *Horae Homileticae*, vol. 21, p. 161.

27. Mounce, *Book of Revelation*, 117.

to heaven and swears by him who lives forever—the one who created all things in both land and sea. The cascade of characteristics grounds this figure in God's self-revelation throughout history: from the beginning of creation to the exodus, and to the end. It carries us into the midst of God's story, shaped throughout the Old Testament (Exodus, Ezekiel, Daniel, the Psalms). It does this to tell us that the story is coming to its fulfillment. The angel proclaims that there will be no more delay—the end has come.

And yet, in the midst of this glorious unveiling, there remains a hiddenness to God: the seven thunders are sealed up—perhaps to hide their meaning from us, perhaps to protect us from their consequences. We don't know. God choses what to reveal of himself. While the angel acknowledges the authority of God, God remains hidden—we hear his voice *from* heaven.

The ethereal language of the book of Revelation seems to lend itself to speculation. We want to figure this out, to discover the hidden secrets. We would like to figure God out—to get a handle on what God is about, particularly in the face of hardship or suffering. It is far too easy to believe that comprehension will bring us confidence. But there is no interpretative key that allows us to make predictions of what is to come or to explain why things happen the way they do. The book of Revelation is not a crystal ball that we might gaze into, but a hymn of praise to the great and terrible God who created all that is and rules over all that is—the God who will complete what he has begun. In the present, we are allowed the luxury of believing that we are rulers in our own right, that we have power, and that we can exert that power in the world. Yet that belief is a luxury which in the end proves disastrous because it blinds us to the truth.

As we go deeper in our theological knowledge, one of the great dangers is that we can begin to put our confidence in our own understanding, in figuring things out, in being able to explain what is happening and why, in becoming *the experts* on God. Who doesn't like being treated with respect in the marketplace or at least in the church? And here, as the seven thunders are silenced, that illusion, that pride, that pompous assumption, is taken away. Instead, this in-breaking of God is a knife that cuts through our pretense and our pretensions to shatter the illusion that we are masters of our fate, the captains of our future, or the ones with insider information. Revelation does not provide us with a secret codebook which will allow us to unpack or predict the future. We are not here to gain knowledge *about* God or to figure God out. We are here to have our eyes and hearts opened to the truth of God, not so that we might grasp God but so that we might be grasped by God.

Revelation 10 anticipates chapter 11, with the seventh trumpet sounding and the declaration that the kingdom of our Lord and his Messiah has arrived (Rev 11:15). And with the twenty-four elders who sit on their thrones before God, we are to fall down and worship God (Rev 11:15, 16). We are here to learn how to worship God with body, soul, heart, and mind, because worship and worship alone is true knowledge of God.

In the opening scene of chapter 10, the magnificent angel is described, and we are told that he holds in his hand a little scroll (Rev 10:2). But it isn't until verse 8 that we return to this little scroll. And it becomes clear that this angel, in all of his magnificence, is a messenger bringing this little scroll to John, who is told to take the scroll from the hand of the angel—to "take and eat" (Rev 10:9).

Echoing Ezekiel's experience (Ezek 3:1–3), John is told that this scroll will be sweet to the taste. It will be sweet to the taste but bitter to the stomach—hard to take in, hard to digest. It is a word from God—it is the word of God, so it cannot help but be sweet. But to a humanity in rebellion against God, it is also bitter. When John obeys, when he "takes and eats" the scroll, it is as sweet as honey but his stomach is in turmoil. John is told to share what he has just consumed. As Ezekiel was told to prophesy to the people of Israel, John "must prophesy [again] about many peoples and nations and languages and kings" (Rev 10:11).

In the face of human suffering and pain and questions about the judgement of God, our hope does not rest in figuring God out or being able to explain "why." It rests on knowing, loving, and worshipping the one who was and is and is to come. Our confidence comes in knowing that from the beginning of the Bible to the end, we have a story that points to a God who is faithful, a God whose purposes have not changed, a God who chooses how he will show himself to us, and a God who gives of himself to redeem us. Take and eat. We receive, we consume the word of God, we consume Christ.[28]

This apocalyptic word breaks into our lives and into our world to liberate us to worship God—to know God. It silences our speculation, draws us in, and gathers us up into the story of God's confrontation of human sinfulness, not to condemn but to redeem. And so, we consume Christ so that with John, we might speak Christ to the world. Our message to the world, our bearing witness to the world, is

28. "John's taking of the little scroll is 'eucharistic,' not in the direct sense that the scene depicts the celebration of the sacrament, but in the sense that he is being commanded to ingest the word of God, to let it enter him so as to become part of his own being" (Mangina, *Revelation*, 132).

not about what we know but about who we are coming to know. And with John, our witness is first and foremost in worship. That we, with the twenty-four elders in Revelation 11:16, might fall on our faces and worship God.

Revelation 8–11

Questions for Further Reflection

1. Read Revelation 8–11.

2. As you are reading, observe the difficult judgments of 9–10 and the response in chapter 10. In what way is worship true knowledge of God?

3. Finally, think about your own response. If you are honest with yourself, what is bittersweet to you about the word of God, theology, or scripture?

7

Standing Fast in the Meantime

Judy Paulsen

When I was sixteen, I was invited by a friend to go with them to their church. The sermon involved the preacher explaining a huge chart that he had on display at the front of the church. It spelled out several great epochs of cosmic history. Images and symbols were given precise explanations. This meant this and that meant that, as the past, present, and future were all neatly mapped out. It was the 70s, when Hal Lindsey's book *The Late Great Planet Earth* remained for twenty weeks on the New York Times Bestseller List. It was the heyday, at least in North America, of something called dispensationalism.

At that point in my life I hadn't yet heard the word "dispensationalism," but even at sixteen, I was skeptical about "the whole chart thing." It seemed unlikely that God's cosmic purpose, and the terrible forces that strove against it, could be so thoroughly known by mere mortals, let alone by a man in a polyester suit and some Bristol board.

It seemed to me then, as it does now, that to strive to so exactly explain both the ancient past and the distant future is just one more example of human grandstanding, evidence of our inability to accept our true place in the order of things. The man with the chart was ultimately an attempt to put God on a chain—domesticating Scripture, and particularly, domesticating a book like Revelation.

But there is, as we have already seen in this sermon series, *another way* to read this book, and that is to allow the Apocalypse (the book's name in Greek) to speak in its own voice, the voice of signs and wonders—images not given to us to stir up explanations but given to stir up wonder, and awe, and obedience. The twelfth chapter, our reading for today, is ripe with potential for this kind of reading, as it focuses on two astonishing antagonists.

The first is a magnificent celestial woman, heavily pregnant, clothed with the sun, wearing a crown of twelve stars, with her feet resting on the moon. We meet her in the throes of labor, that perilous time of both great pain and great promise (Rev 12:1–2). Harry Boer, missionary theologian to Nigeria, writes, "She is the OT community of the faithful that climaxes in the motherhood of Mary."[29] Eve, the People of Israel, Mary, Mother Church all rolled into one. Sounds like the kind of image a timeless God would dream up.

But now enters her horrific foe, a great red dragon/ serpent figure seeking to devour her newborn child and wage war on her. He is formidable and threatening: the devourer, the accuser, hating the good, seeking to destroy, coming with an army of fallen angels (Rev 12:3–4). New Testament scholar William Barclay describes this as "the power of evil ever watching for its opportunity to frustrate the upward reach of man."[30]

29. Boer, *Book of Revelation*, 89.
30. Barclay, *Revelation of John*, vol. 2, 78.

Time in this passage is strangely both collapsed and extended; the ancient past, present, and future are jumbled together. We read of the oddly specific 1260 days and the weirdly non-specific "time, and times, and half a time" (Rev 12:14). There is both a powerful tension and connection between the supernatural and natural world, the cosmic and earthly, the timely and timeless. But at the heart of it all is the kingdom of God and the authority of his Messiah.

Although the passage clearly points to humans contending with the Enemy, this passage is obviously *not about us*. We are bit players in this cosmic battle. First and foremost, this passage is a picture of the majesty, salvation, and power of God:

- who catches up the threatened child to his very throne (12:5)

- whose archangel and angels contend with and defeat the Devil (12:7–8)

- who expels Satan from heaven (12:9)

- who conquers him by the blood of the Lamb (12:11)

- who provides a timely place of refuge for the woman (12:16)

The passage makes it so clear that this is no battle of equally matched forces of good and evil. As Joseph Mangina has written, the serpent dragon *has no power* to harm either the child or its mother. Its only recourse is to tirelessly deceive and accuse—the serpent is the original bearer of false witness.[31]

Although already conquered, this hideous foe is determined to use his remaining time to make war on the rest of the woman's children. This is where we come in.

31. Mangina, *Revelation*, 154.

For if the woman is the mother of the Messiah, we Christ-followers are also her offspring. And the passage makes it clear that our task is one of simple obedience: to keep God's commandments and to hold the testimony of Jesus (Rev 12:11, 17). No matter the cost. No matter the false accusations, threats, isolation, or persecution. Even unto death. We are to point by both our words and deeds to the great saving work of God made known in Jesus. We are simply to stand fast in the meantime, this in-between time, when the Devil has been conquered and disarmed, but not yet bound. And be sure of this—he is not yet bound.

Who can say why God didn't finish the job? Certainly not us. All we're told is that the final battle has already been won and we've been given our marching orders: keep the commandments of God and hold the testimony of Jesus (Rev 12:17). As people training for leadership in the Church, this passage suggests we cannot expect an easy time of it. The disarmed accuser is still as mad as hell.

There will be days when our great foe will whisper in your ear, "The Church—it's nothing more than people jockeying for power and building empires. It's all a house of cards." *Hold* to the testimony of Jesus that says, "I will build my Church and the gates of hell will not prevail against it" (Matt 16:18).

There will be days when he screams at you, "What are you doing? Throwing your life away on a job that is long on hours and short on any real gains." *Hold* to the testimony of Jesus that says, "You will receive power when the Holy Spirit comes on you, and you will be my witnesses in Jerusalem, in all Judea and Samaria, and to the ends of the earth" (Acts 1:8).

There will be days when Satan will sit across from you and calmly state, "You're all alone in this mess—no one cares about the budget that's in the red, or the broken boiler, or the sermon you'll preach on Sunday." *Hold* to the testimony of Jesus that says, "Come to me all who are weary and heavy laden and I will give you rest" (Matt 11:28), and especially "I am with you always to the very end of the age" (Matt 28:20).

Keep the commandments of God and hold the testimony of Jesus. In other words, witness by word and deed but don't expect an easy ride. In the end, as Julian of Norwich once said, "All shall be well, and all shall be well and all manner of thing shall be well."[32] But *that* story is for another day and another chapter . . .

Revelation 12

Questions for Further Reflection

1. The words "revelation" and "apocalypse" are used in a variety of ways in society today. Do an online search of the origin and meaning of these two words.

2. Read Revelation 12 in its entirety. How does the power of evil compare to the power of God? What does that mean for you in your everyday life?

3. When you read the phrase "testimony of Jesus," what comes to mind for you? What does it look like for you to "hold to the testimony of Jesus" in the midst of the challenges in your life?

32. Graves, "All Shall Be Well."

8

Reading Babylon from the Margins

David Kupp

As a human species, we have a mixed history with our cities—their rise, their fall, and (sometimes) their revival. Those who have studied our once great and now collapsed civilizations list ancient Sumer and Egypt among them, followed by early empires across India, China, Mexico, Peru, and parts of Europe by 1000 BCE.[33] At the heart of each of these civilizations stood one or more ancient capitals, often tiny by contemporary standards. Many today may be no more than ruins, populated by memories, ghosts, archaeologists, and perhaps tourists. Some ancient cities outlived their first founders, however, and became viable once again, displaying multiple lives and forms. Rome, of course, is an example of this: a first-century urban empire capital of giant proportions for its time, with perhaps a half-million residents.[34] Over the past two millennia, it has

33. See Wright's overview of these early civilizations: Wright, *Short History of Progress*, 55ff.

34. Apparently straightforward questions like the population of the ancient city of Rome remain difficult to resolve. For example, see Turchin *et al.*, "Coin Hoards Speak of Population Declines," 17276–79.

cycled through flourishing, convulsing, and re-emerging. Revelation 18 describes what appears to be one of those convulsions of Rome, in a mix of proleptic history, fantastical prophecy, and divine analogy. This is the story of Rome headed for collapse, and about to make way for the New Jerusalem.

In this collection of meditations upon the book of Revelation, we have become aware of numerous aspects of John's remarkable apocalypse. Several deserve reconsideration here—for their particular influence on readings of chapter 18, and by virtue of the book of Revelation's complicated history of readings.

Revelation 18 sits as the capstone judgement piece in a book that is difficult to understand, interpret, and preach. It has enough visions, symbols, numerology, surreal beasts, and sea monsters to rival the best science fiction imagery. Out of the sixty-six books in the Christian Scriptures, probably none has provoked more emotions, more readings or mis-readings, or more controversy.

As a vision of swift and total urban judgement, chapter 18 employs the multi-genre nature of the book as a whole: an "apocalypse"—that is, a "disclosure"—that comes in the form of a circular letter, and that delivers at numerous points prophetic oracles. This multi-genre combination is itself a paradox—the book is written as an open letter to be heard in multiple Christian gatherings, even while it employs the hidden language of apocalyptic symbol and myth, rather than descriptive narrative or theological appeal and reasoning.

It is notable that chapter 18 reinforces why John's Apocalypse has had a rough ride attaining canonical status. From its earliest appearance, Revelation seems to have had difficulty securing and holding its place in the canon, according to numerous commentators.

- In the third century, Presbyter Gaius of Rome (ca. 210 CE) and Bishop Dionysius of Alexandria (ca. 250 CE) treated it with suspicion.

- In the fourth century, Cyril of Jerusalem (315–386 CE) forbade its public and private reading.

- Chrysostom and Eusebius were not clear whether Revelation belonged in the biblical canon.

- At one point, Martin Luther said that Revelation is "neither apostolic nor prophetic . . . My spirit cannot accommodate itself to this book . . . I stick to the books which present Christ to me clearly and purely."[35]

- John Calvin wrote a commentary on every other book in the New Testament except Revelation.

- The Eastern Orthodox lectionary does not include any readings from Revelation; and Anglicans and Catholics are minimalists on that score.

Chapter 18 contributes as well to the vast theatre of speculation about John's Apocalypse—by preachers, authors, interpreters, filmmakers, and musicians. In the previous meditation, Judy Paulsen referenced Hal Lindsay's 1970s blockbuster *The Late Great Planet Earth*, to which I might add my own teenage band's pathetic attempts to cover numerous Larry Norman and Randy Stonehill songs. And, of course, we cannot overlook America's bestseller in the popular apocalyptic genre, Jerry B. Jenkins and his co-author Tim LaHaye, who have turned the *Left Behind* fiction series into a multi-million dollar enterprise (and into

35. Luther, "Preface to the Revelation of St. John," 398–99.

a controversy that currently stalks the venerable Moody Bible Institute). Wikipedia lists over 200 separate website pages in the category of "Post-Apocalyptic Video Games." Some of these games draw directly (if loosely) from John's Apocalypse . . . "I wish we'd all been ready." Add to this the current apocalyptic and zombie fixation of popular media.

Whether the entertainment world's saturation with apocalyptic images makes the church's contemporary engagement of Revelation or other Scriptures more or less difficult is worth consideration. In a world where a 12- to 15-year-old gamer might spend a dozen or more hours weekly inside a highly interactive and detailed post-apocalyptic virtual reality, the ability to receive other forms of input (like, perhaps, the reception of a sedately read biblical text on Sunday morning) may be hampered.

Against the background of these alternative readings and images that vie for our attention, we turn to the pages of Revelation 18. Chapter 18 sits at the heart of two and a half chapters on Babylon and her destiny. Chapter 17 laid out the vision of the woman and the scarlet beast and the angel's interpretation, and Chapter 18 hammers us straight between the eyes with the unflinching judgement of Babylon. (Or between the ears, if we keep in mind the scenario of John's Apocalypse read live and dramatically in the congregation, from one end of the manuscript to the other.)

17:1–19:10 Babylon and her destiny

17:1–7 The vision of the woman and the scarlet beast

17:8–18 The angel's interpretation

18:1–19:9 The judgment of Babylon

18:1–3 The bright angel's announcement

18:4–20 The voice from heaven

18:21–24 The angel with the millstone

19:1–8 The rejoicing of heaven and earth

19:9–10 John and the angel

We can view this entire scene as a cosmic courtroom drama which pits the earth's greatest empire city against the cries of its victims. As Elizabeth Schüssler Fiorenza describes it, the earthly splendor, wealth, and power of Rome-as-Babylon meet the heavenly splendor and power of God as presiding judge.[36] A class-action suit has been brought by Christians, together with all those killed on the earth (Rev 18:24). The charge against Rome-as-Babylon is murder, for the sake of its own power and idolatry. The divine judgement, already announced (Rev 14:8), is reiterated (Rev 18:2–3): Rome-as-Babylon has lost the lawsuit, and its true foulness is exposed. Its associates break out in lamentation and mourning, while the heavenly court and Christians rejoice over the justice they have received. In the sentence against Rome-as-Babylon, they have won their complaint and satisfied their claims to justice. The divine court commissions the beast and the ten horns to execute the sentence.

In a few phrases, the story has shifted dramatically from Revelation 17's picture of the magnificent Rome-as-Babylon flaunting its wealth and power, to a scene of catastrophe where:

- the great heavenly angel announces Babylon's fall (18:1–3)

- a new heavenly narrator cries out a warning, "Come out of her, my people," in a double prophetic oracle (18:4–5, 6–8)

- a series of dirges and lamentations arise over Rome-as-Babylon (18:9–19).

36. Schüssler Fiorenza, *Book of Revelation*, 7; and *Revelation: Vision of a Just World*, 99.

These climax in a prophetic call of praise (which at the same time points forward to the concluding hymns in Chapter 19:1–8). The sign-action of the millstone heaved into the ocean ends the chapter, and a summary statement of Rome's indictment: its crime was murder.

Whatever you think or feel about cities and about urban life, at this point, John's account of Babylon's judgement warrants some meta-reflection. We are today, after all, an urban species—even more profoundly than the people of John's Apocalypse. At the heart of this text, I read an urban dualism: the great contrast between Babylon and the New Jerusalem. And it is a true dualism: John is an extremist here, allowing for very limited continuity or overlap between the two cities.

The fall of Babylon leaves us gasping; it is portrayed as the near-instant collapse of empire, as monarchy, markets, and immorality suddenly lie smoking in a pile of decadent rot. "Foul! Filthy!" (Rev 18:2) shouts the angel again and again. Then the heavenly narrator jumps in: "Get out while you can!!" (Rev 18:4). And suddenly, we are back for a moment in Egypt, with pestilence and plagues and fire in the unmitigated dissolution of an empire capital. Babylon's friends and business partners, the kings, the merchants, and the sailors stand aghast and weep.

How are we to absorb this sight, this pain, this desolation? Are we to protest like Abraham over Sodom: "Will you sweep away the righteous with the wicked?" (Gen 18:16–33). When they heard this dramatic liturgical performance, what was the expected role of the first Christian audiences to this apocalypse? Did they do as bidden, and cheer, stomp, and applaud? Did they weep and shout for their relatives and friends who they imagine might not make it out of Babylon? Did they take on the attitude of Abraham and protest the harshness of the judgement?

At a certain point in my international development work, I was given a new assignment, to gather a team and explore the phenomenon of urban poverty and development in both the global South and North. We spent many months walking the favelas and slums and shanty towns of the cities around the world—listening, gathering stories, observing, in places like Bangkok, Kolkata, Delhi, Los Angeles, Nairobi, Phnom Penh, Johannesburg, Addis Ababa, Dakar, and Chicago. On rainy days, we squelched through rivers of human excrement flowing down pathways. We begged permission from drug lords with *pistolas* in hand to enter their favelas. Our team interviewed girl-child prostitutes, and their traffickers. We listened to stories from slum pastors, priests, and imams. We visited HIV clinics, child-headed households, and habitat initiatives. We heard pitches from eager entrepreneurs building new enterprises with enormous creativity and energy.

It was one of the richest, most humbling experiences of our lives. You can imagine the cascade of learning, amidst our admiration for some of the bravest, most talented people we'd ever encountered. Among the many lessons, let me leave you with one. We learned that the poor read the Scriptures from the margins, in ways that you and I in the top billion do not comprehend. We discovered people in every slum with deep dignity and resilience. We discovered people with a passion for well-being. They wanted the downfall of their Babylon, those structures that hoard power and block revolutionary change. We learned that God was in their city, in their slum; God had always been there. There is not a slum, not a shack, not a market kiosk, not a tented refugee city where the triune God—Father, Son, and Holy Spirit—is not embedded.

John tells us that the city can be hell or the city can be a crucible for transformation. When the city is hell, or Babylon, and you are on its margins and under its thumb, you will rejoice when it is gone. When the city is a place of good news, a New Jerusalem being discovered, then even slums can generate urban communities of hope. At minimum, Revelation 18 is a call for all Christians, from the first to the twenty-first century, to "Wake up!" and "Get out while you can!" We are sleepwalking through our cities of Babylon without any sense that we are in any particular danger.

One final, sobering question that Revelation 18 might leave us with: how is it possible for you and I, as the new kings and merchants of the planet, to hear this Apocalypse drama? In fact, who in our world perhaps views us as the Babylon in John's Apocalypse? We, as global north Christians, have joined forces with the top billion (yes, Canada—in the G7, in OECD, with our power, our resources, our weapons of war, our control of global finance). We have built a global empire of vassals to meet our every demand:

- Our merchants scour the earth every day for us.

- Our kings deliver any pearl or bauble to us by courier and drone.

- Our vassals ship kiwis and strawberries and Kobe beef to us in winter from every corner of the earth.

Are we recreating Babylon on a global scale? And in that vast commodification of life so available to us by our hands on the levers of globalization and wealth, do we cease to need the triune, cosmic, and immanent God, aside from our emotional sustenance and support, and detached theological coherence? How does Revelation 18 read us, and our city? May God make us uncomfortable in Babylon, and worthy of the New Jerusalem.

Revelation 18

Questions for Further Reflection

1. In your reading of Revelation 18, what do you see that looks like our own cities? In what way are we Babylon? In what way are we the New Jerusalem, or in what way can we become the Holy City?

2. What aspects of our own neighborhoods and faith communities' worldviews and behaviors are challenged by Revelation's condemnation of the practices of Babylon?

3. Can you imagine what it would be like to read Revelation from the margins—as someone who is oppressed and powerless? Would the images in Revelation of judgment and the destruction of the powerful be an encouragement?

9

Is God Violent? Implications for Christians

MURRAY HENDERSON

IS THE CHRISTIAN GOD violent? Many people in the modern world hold that the Christian faith, its Scriptures, and its God are inherently violent and that the church of the crucified Messiah breeds violence on the earth. The collective historical memory of Europe and her former colonies following the Reformation is that of Christians who slaughtered each other in the name of the Lamb of God.

Throughout the revelation of God to John of Patmos, God battles against the destroyers of the earth: Satan, the dragon, the beast and false prophet, and Babylon, the whore. In Revelation 11:18, the twenty-four elders fall on their faces in worship to God, and proclaim that the time has come for the wrath of God to destroy those who destroy the earth. In Chapter 18, the angel proclaims that Babylon the whore—the Roman empire—has fallen. She is the center of *porneia*—of sexual immorality—and the kings and merchants of the earth have committed fornication with her and grown rich from the power of her luxury (Rev 18:1–3). Babylon is guilty of the blood of the saints of God (Rev 18:24). In one hour, the judgment of God has fallen upon the city once idolized as the great city of the world (Rev 18:10). Unbridled luxury, political and economic injustice, sexual immorality, and the refusal to accept the living God are the marks of the city's iniquity. These marks bear an eerie similarity to aspects of the modern and post-modern world.

In Chapter 19 we are introduced to a great multitude praising God (Rev 19:1). The worshippers are the twenty-four elders, the four living creatures, the servants of Yahweh, and all who fear him, great and small. These heavenly worshippers give us a glimpse of the future in which God alone establishes justice. The worshippers praise God first for the destruction of Babylon/Rome. Smoke rises from the city forever—the demonstration that this center of evil will never recover (Rev 19:1–5). Second, the worshippers praise God for the long-awaited marriage of the Lamb to his bride the Church (Rev 19:6–8)—the Lamb who is at the center of the throne, the savior of those victimized by Satan and his cohort, who will wipe away every tear from the eyes of those who have suffered unjustly (Rev 7:17). Four great "hallelujahs" issue forth like the sound of many waters and mighty thunder peals. The portrayal of the splendor and extravagance of heavenly worship is likely intended by John as a model for his struggling churches.

The angel instructs John to write, "Blessed are those who are invited to the marriage supper of the Lamb" (Rev 19:9). The Lamb's bride is ready, clothed appropriately in fine white linen—the righteous deeds which, in God's grace, they have been empowered to perform. White linens, a white stone (Rev 2:17), and a white horse—white, the color of righteousness. And so John prepares us for the account of this great marriage and the feast to follow.

But wait, instead, the heavens open and a rider on a white horse, whose name is Faithful and True, rides into battle. He is the Word of God, and his robes are dipped in blood—his own blood once offered at Calvary (Rev 19:11–16). He is inscribed with one name which only he knows, a reminder that while the Church's knowledge of God is sufficient for salvation, the Church's knowledge is not exhaustive. Revelation does not dissolve mystery. From the mouth of this rider comes a sharp sword with which he will rule the nations of the earth. Oddly, perhaps, there is no battle scene. No military action is ascribed to the armies which follow God's Messiah on their white horses. The sharp sword from the mouth of the Word of God establishes his sovereign authority over the earth. This sword alone is counted worthy to pour out God's wrath upon those who have followed Satan. We are tempted to say, "Well, this isn't really violence. It's just a word." But this is the mighty Word which brings Creation into Being. And there is another great supper spread, not that of the Messiah's wedding, but a supper in which the birds feast upon the Satanic destroyers of the earth. The beast and false prophet are captured and thrown into the lake of fire. The rest of Satan's followers are killed by the sword from the mouth of the rider on the white horse (Rev 19:17–21).

So how, if at all, do we reconcile the figure of the Lamb slaughtered for the sin of the world with the rider on the white horse who treads the winepress of the fury of the wrath of God the Almighty? Miroslav Volf argues against a "god" who would act "as if" sin does not exist. By contrast, to affirm the identity of the Lamb and the rider on a white horse is to refuse to pretend that the world is already redeemed.[37] God's patience with the destroyers is

37. Volf, *Exclusion and Embrace*, 294.

great, but it has its limits. Every delay in God bringing in the consummation is a time of the continued suffering of the saints and the innocent. That's why the Church is an Advent community, praying every day, "Amen, Come Lord Jesus."

It seems to me that God's revelation to the Seer of Patmos provides us with materials for a Christian theology of history which the Church badly needs today. World history is the scene of warring spiritual forces, those of God and those of the powers of darkness. The battle is not against flesh and blood, but "against the spiritual forces of evil in the heavenly places" (Eph 6:12). The culmination of God's Kingdom is revealed as eschatological—an achievement of God and his Messiah at the end of world history. While the wounded Lamb invites all to come to salvation through his blood, God *must* pronounce judgement upon those who insist on being beasts and false prophets, followers of Satan, destroyers of the earth. A God who smiles benignly at the atrocities of Auschwitz, Rwanda, Syria, Myanmar, failing to unleash his anger at the perpetuators, is unworthy of worship. In the light of the revelation given to John of Patmos, such a non-indignant God can only be considered a figment of the liberal imagination.

But here is the critical point: the rider on the white horse demonstrates that violence is rightly the monopoly of the biblical God. We, his followers, are to take up our crosses to follow the crucified Messiah. We are to eschew violence and pursue peace as best we can. Only God can be trusted with a judgment which is both just and an aspect of God's love. Human justice has shown itself to be, at best, exceedingly rough. God's justice alone is righteous. Our human attempts to exercise violence in the pursuit of justice always end in the victims soon coming to resemble the former oppressors. Of course, systems of proximate human justice are necessary. However, they are inevitably flawed by human self-interest.

John of Patmos provides us with a vision which completes the eschatological vision of the Gospels and St. Paul. Miroslav Volf states, "The certainty of God's just judgement at the end of history is the presupposition for the renunciation of violence in the middle of it."[38] Certain that God will deal with the destroyers of the earth and its people, the church of the crucified Lamb is absolutely set free to renounce violence in all its forms, and to work for peace. There can be no New Jerusalem on earth, no consummation of the Kingdom inaugurated by Jesus Christ, without the justice of God first having been delivered against all who refuse the embrace of the Lamb. We are to take up our crosses and follow the Lamb, in this time between the times, allowing God to be God, trusting God and his Messiah to do justice in the end, and praying every day, "Even so, Come, Lord Jesus."

Revelation 18–19

Questions for Further Reflection

1. Read Revelation 18–19 closely, noticing what God does and what humans do.

2. Do you agree that certainty about God's judgment allows for the renunciation of violence?

3. How does the book of Revelation shape your theology about atrocities like Auschwitz, Rwanda, Syria, and Myanmar? In what way would a Bible without

38. Ibid., 302.

the book of Revelation or some description of God's judgment be lacking?

10

He Will Come Again to Judge the Living and the Dead

Thomas P. Power

Chapter 20 of the Book of Revelation has been the subject of numerous tomes speculating, for instance, on one of its central elements, i.e. the meaning of the thousand years. We have a natural curiosity about matters like the return of Christ before or after the millennium, and it makes an interesting study to see how different groups down the centuries have interpreted it. However, whether pre-millennialist, post-millennialist, or amillenialist, historic and contemporary fixations upon the meaning of the millennium should not obscure the spiritual riches and assurances of the chapter. In this short meditation, I will highlight what Revelation 20 tells us about the character of God and our situation as believers, here and now, and for the future, focusing upon God's sovereignty, justice, judgment, and grace.

The Sovereignty of God

Right through the book of Revelation, there is a battle between the forces of evil and God and his people. The conclusion of that battle comes in this chapter, which has the tenor of finality, expressed in conflict and judgment, victory and defeat, life and death, the saved and the lost, all configured around the theme of hope, which is pivotal to the book as a whole.

It is in this battle that God's sovereignty is clearly expressed, and here, specifically in his disposal of Satan. How does this happen? It occurs in two stages: his binding and his destruction. Satan is already bound in a sense, for with Christ's first coming, the kingdom of God has come, and Jesus went around casting out evil spirits to demonstrate precisely this (2 Thess 2:1–2). And we know that Satan was defeated on the cross and with the resurrection of Jesus. His final defeat awaits.

First, he is bound and consigned to an abyss, like a prison sentence, for a thousand years. (Rev 20:1–3). This period of confinement is not just random, for as we know, in Revelation, numbers are usually symbolic. Here, the number one thousand, a cube of ten, is a number of completeness. In other words, Satan is bound for a perfect period. As well as a perfect period of confinement, notable also is Satan's insignificance in the whole drama. This is indicated by the fact that it is not the Father or Christ who carries out this act of binding; but in an act of delegation, the task is left to an anonymous angel. A final aspect of Satan's confinement is that, in contrast to the present age when he is still active, his activities are completely controlled or limited for the duration of his binding. So, the sovereignty of God is evident in Satan's perfect period of confinement, his insignificance, and the limitation on his activities, all indicative that the end is under God's control.

This binding up of Satan should likely be taken symbolically. But what, we must ask, is the point of binding? What purpose does it serve? Why does God not get rid of Satan right away? As verse 3 tells us, the purpose of binding is "to keep him from deceiving the nations any more until the thousand years were ended." But there is an additional purpose.

Again, answering the question, "What is the point of binding?" we note that following his release after confinement, Satan shows no sign of change, for he goes back to his old ways and gathers the forces of evil for a final showdown. Though still under God's control, Satan will lead the wicked in one final act of rebellion and try to destroy God's people. He resumes his evil ways, but this time on a larger scale (Rev 20:7–9). All this is evidence that restraining evil even for a complete or perfect period is not sufficient. Doing so only proves that evil is relentless and unchanging.

This occasions God's second, final act against Satan—his destruction. The nations during his binding are not deceived by Satan, but upon his release, they give in, showing that whenever Satan is active, people succumb. He gathers the nations for a final battle, epitomized in Gog and Magog, who symbolize the forces of evil—the enemies of God's people. But by this point, God has had enough. Quickly and decisively the forces of evil are assembled and judged. But there is no final battle! God simply decides to act and succeeds. Evil is decimated by fire from heaven without a battle, despite the vast scale and apparently limitless force assembled (Rev 20:9–10).

And so, God exercises his authority, power, and sovereignty against Satan, emanating in his destruction and the destruction of all who follow him. This is the Satan who has, as the prince of this world, accused us, deceived us, denied us peace, love, and security; brought in their place distrust, rebellion, and fear of death; and who has sought and gained for himself the worship which belongs to God alone. God now casts Satan into the lake of fire, where he will suffer for ever with the beast and the false prophet. He is now gone for all time. Satan will no longer lurk, accuse, deceive, or condemn. The forces of evil unleashed by Satan into society to corrupt its social, political, and economic functions are eliminated. God frees the world from these forces that spoil human existence. Evil is done with forever! Its defeat is real and certain. God, not evil, rules the world and its destiny (Isa 24:21–23).

Justice of God

Another significant aspect of the binding of Satan is that the Christian martyrs are recognized. Who are they? We are told in verse 4 that they are "the souls of those who had been beheaded because of their testimony for Jesus and because of the word of God. They had not worshiped the beast or his image and had not received his mark on their foreheads or their hands." What happens to them? In an act of divine justice, they are raised to life again and they come to share in the blessings of Christ's kingdom for a thousand years—again, the perfect, complete time, coinciding with the term of Satan's confinement. In a supreme act of restoration and justice, this becomes the first resurrection, the raising of the martyrs to a life of glory with Christ. Raised, they will not die again, nor will they be judged, but will reign with Christ (Rev 20:4–6).

Judgment of God

On March 3, 2018, in Hamilton, a group of thirty hooded anarchists vandalized shops and businesses in protest against gentrification, causing over $100,000 worth of damage. The community felt violated, but the culprits eluded capture. Following the incident, there was anger that such thugs could seemingly get away with acts so destructive to others. At the same time, much good that occurs in the city of Hamilton goes unnoticed: there is the True City movement where churches act together for the good of the city; a thriving arts sector exemplifying new creativity in a post-industrial area; and proactive efforts to welcome refugees. No doubt such efforts could be cited for other cities. What are we to think? On the one hand, callous acts are committed all the time; and on the other, acts of charity and sacrifice go unrecognized.

When we read Revelation 20 in light of the injustice and lack of recognition of the good that is done, we can thank God for judgment of human actions, good and bad. For here, we see all the dead being raised to appear before the throne of God for judgment. No one can avoid judgment, irrespective of status. As Scripture tells us: "for we must all appear before the judgment seat of Christ, that each one may receive what is due him for the things done while in the body, whether good or bad" (2 Cor 5:10).

Drawing on an older Jewish tradition that all our human actions are recorded in a heavenly book, chapter 20 introduces the books of deeds in which all our acts are recorded and for which we are to be held accountable (Rev 20:11–15). The fact that actions are recorded means that what we do matters to God, and we are accountable. The message given here is that we should continue to do right, perform charitable acts, and serve those in need, even if this brings no recognition. And at the same time, the existence of the books of deeds is an indication that in the end injustice will be brought to account.

Grace of God

While deeds or actions matter, John makes it clear that we are not saved by what we do. Rather, it is on the basis of God's grace that judgment will be conducted. That is the purpose of the book of life. Again, drawing on Hebrew tradition, the book of life records the names of those who have eternal life (Esth 6:1–2; Dan 7:10). In it are the names of citizens of the city of God, the New Jerusalem. Their names are already there, not by their own efforts or by their actions, but by divine grace. We are told that these names are there from the beginning of the world, but not because they are those who have done good deeds. They are there because God decided to include them as an act of grace.

This would make it seem as if God has chosen some people for everlasting life and not others—some are in and others are not. And it makes God seem unfair. All of this seems contrary to the message of hope Revelation wishes to convey. As we see in chapter 21, which follows, the numbers entering the gates of the New Jerusalem seem like a torrent rather than a trickle.

In the view of one commentator on this chapter, it seems to point to a paradox in the whole judgment exercise. On the one hand, the books of deeds imply that our actions matter and that we will be held accountable for them. On the other hand, the book of life suggests that people are not saved by what they do but by the grace of

God.[39] Ultimately, our actions do matter because they impact those around us, yet in the end, the message of this chapter is that salvation and the future is a gift from God, graciously given to those whom God chooses.

Chapter 20 of Revelation sets before us a magnificent but daunting series of word pictures delineating key characteristics of God's nature: God's majesty as judge and God's grace as loving father. By giving us this vision of the future, we are called to a commitment, but not in the way proposed by those who take an obsessive interest in trying to read the predictions of Revelation into the present or project them into the future, epitomized in the entire politico-religious culture that is built around them. As history shows, speculations about the millennium are ultimately uncertain. We are to allow judgment and its timing to be in God's hands. What is certain is the defeat of evil, the judgment of God, justice, and grace, all of which are meant to evoke trust, faith, and hope.

Instead, we are called in the present to a renewed commitment to do as Micah 6:8 instructs: "To act justly, to love mercy and to walk humbly with your God." We are to embrace a living faith in Jesus Christ reflected in a discipleship that impacts all areas of our lives: the everyday decisions of life, how we conduct our relationships, our commitments, and how we use our time. And to do so even if others don't notice, all done in the knowledge that we are accountable to God alone, and also in the knowledge that current forms of injustice and oppression will one day end.

With its message of hope, Revelation 20 acts as an incentive to persevere in faith, not to fear evil, and gives an assurance that our longings for justice will be fulfilled through God's justice and judgment. Let us thank God that

39. Koester, *Revelation and the End of All Things*, 190–91.

our future is greater than we can imagine. Let us place our trust in God regarding our future, confident that God is in control of all eternity, knowing that the outcome is certain. Let us join with angels around the throne in saying: "Praise and glory and wisdom and thanks and honor and power and strength to our God for ever and ever! Amen" (Rev 7:12).

Revelation 20

Questions for Further Reflection

1. Why is a final judgment necessary? Read Revelation 20, taking note of the purpose and outcome of the final judgment.

2. Read 1 John 4:16–18. If you feel an element of fear about the final judgment, how does this passage help to allay those fears?

3. How should a knowledge of the final judgment affect your life now? How might it impact you in relation to the need for forgiveness, justice in the world, faithfulness and good works, repentance, and evangelism?

11

The Tree of Life

CATHERINE SIDER HAMILTON

> The tree of life my soul hath seen,
> Laden with fruit and always green;
> The trees of nature fruitless be
> Compared with Christ the apple tree.[40]

THE SONG IS HAUNTING and beautiful—beautiful because
it speaks of Christ our life; haunting because it sings him
here, in this time. And in this, it speaks to the beautiful and
haunting book of Revelation:

> And [the angel] showed me the river of the wa-
> ter of life sparkling like crystal, flowing out from
> the throne of God and of the Lamb. In the midst
> of its street and the river on either side, the tree
> of life bearing twelve fruits, each month yield-
> ing its fruit, and the leaves of the tree are for the
> healing of the nations (Rev 22:1).[41]

---

40. Smith, "Tree of Life." See Mangina, *Revelation*, 247, who also
links this song with Revelation 22.

41. The translations of Revelation are my own.

This is the "city of God and of the Lamb." Here, at the end of the waste and havoc wreaked through so many of Revelation's twenty-two chapters, after Gog and Magog and their swarming hosts, after the cruel and scarlet city, after the beast and the false prophet and Satan himself—that ancient serpent—and after all the people branded with his name, wearing the rule of the beast on their forehead like some kind of twisted tephillin—after all this, out of the chaos of fire, now, at last, the holy city comes:

> And I saw a new heaven and a new earth, for the first heaven and the first earth had passed away and the sea was no longer. And the holy city, the new Jerusalem I saw coming down out of heaven from God (Rev 21:1).

It is a city to tear the heart, for its beauty is beyond compare: "her radiance like the most precious stone, like a jasper shining" (Rev 21:11); her twelve gates each a great pearl; her foundations studded with sapphire and emerald, amethyst, beryl and topaz, and jewels we do not even know. This golden city is lit by the glory of God, "and its light is the Lamb" (Rev 21:23). It is a city to tear the heart, for its beauty is beyond compare, and at its center is the Lamb.

"The Lamb": this is Revelation's preferred title for Jesus, the one who sits upon the throne, the one who is and who was and who is to come, Alpha and Omega, the beginning and the end. This one reigns at the center of the New Jerusalem, and it is for this reason that the city shines.

For Jerusalem, the city of God's people, has not always shone. "*Eichah!*" Lamentations cries, "Alas! How solitary sits the city that once was full of people . . . in the street the sword bereaves; in the house it is like death" (Lam 1:1, 20). Alas for the holy city! "Her uncleanness was in her skirts;

her downfall was appalling . . . she has even seen the nations invade her sanctuary" (Lam 1:10). Alas! "Jerusalem has sinned grievously," the city herself cries. "Look and see if there is any sorrow like my sorrow" (Lam 1:12).

There is another city that comes before the holy city, as both Revelation and Lamentations know. Call it "Babylon"; call it "Jerusalem"; call it "the church." There is another city, and it is not a city that shines. Pray for the people *"who walk in darkness, who chose* thee *and oppose* thee."[42] There is a city that turns away from God and from his throne, that hears another word, an ancient word, a pleasant word: "Did God say 'You shall not eat? . . . You will not die, but you will be as gods" (Gen 3:1, 5). This is the city that hears a word that captures and compels our ears: you will be as gods! No need for God, no time for the Word, no need for *his* good; let us construct our own.

T. S. Eliot knew this city:

Where shall the word be found, where will the word
Resound? Not here, there is not enough silence . . .
The right time and the right place are not here
No place of grace for those who avoid the face
No time to rejoice for those who walk among noise and
deny the voice.[43]

Alas! How lonely sits the city.

Revelation is haunting because it is true. It knows the desolation of the city that does not hear the word that is its life. The holy city has a precursor in that other city, lost and weeping in its chosen exile. "Jerusalem, Jerusalem," Jesus cries (Matt 23:37). In the midst of the city of God's people he weeps, and he walks on the path we have made

42. T. S. Eliot, "Ash Wednesday V," 102–3.
43. Ibid., 102.

for ourselves, and on the cross he rises, with us and for us and in our place.

"The tree of life my soul hath seen." There is a tree in the midst of the holy city. It has the shape of a great and suffering love. "Is it nothing to you, all you who pass by? Look and see if there is any sorrow like my sorrow" (Lam 1:12).

Revelation answers Jerusalem's lament. God does see, and his judgement is also and finally his love. That the city of God's people should no longer be a filthy thing, all her precious things defiled. That we should shine like gold; that we should be again a holy people in the city of our God. This is the will of God. This is the heart of God, who so loved the world that he sent his only Son.

"And I saw the heavenly city, the new Jerusalem, coming down out of heaven like a bride made ready for her husband, in the beauty of holiness, radiant at the sight of her beloved" (Rev 21:2). It is the radiance of joy. There is no pearl large enough to describe this joy; all the jewels in the world cannot contain it. It is the radiance of the New Jerusalem—God's people lifted up in the arms of the Lamb to look on the face of their Lord again.

Our God does not leave his people alone. Even in the place of the skull his love rises—his love, the Lamb, our life. "And he showed me the river of the water of life sparkling like crystal, flowing out from the throne of God and of the Lamb" (Rev 22:1). There, in the midst of the city, the Lamb. He is for us the tree of life, taking that other tree on his back, carrying its terrible cost through the streets of the unholy city on his own back. The tree of life my soul has seen. The whole vision of Revelation, the whole sweep of the biblical narrative comes to a point on this tree. It is our beginning and our end, the Alpha and the Omega. In the tree by our own choice our dying. On the tree by his great love our life. Jesus Christ, "the apple tree," that we might live and sing again.

At the end of the story there is the song: the city that may be called holy again, the city of God not forgotten but cleansed. And I saw the holy city, the New Jerusalem, coming down out of heaven from God and from the Lamb. It is Israel's city, and ours. Its radiance is ours, God's people made ready in the love of the Lamb, God's people made ready in the blood of the Lamb, to cleave to him. So that we might no longer hide; so that we might no longer weep, naked and ashamed and sovereign in the lonely city. That we might cleave to him as we were meant to cleave in the beginning of creation.

He calls to us. In his body and his blood he gives himself to us; with all that he is and all that he has he honors us, that we might turn and cleave to him. It is the marriage supper of the Lamb.

> The tree of life my soul has seen
> Laden with fruit and always green.
> The trees of nature fruitless be
> Compared with Christ the apple tree.[44]

Amen.

Revelation 21–22:5

Questions for Further Reflection

1. The sermon links three "cities"—Babylon, Jerusalem, and the Church—and calls them the precursors of the holy city. In what ways do you think these cities

44. Smith, "Tree of Life."

are similar? What does the coming of the holy city, the "New Jerusalem" mean for the other cities? How are they related in the time of the New Jerusalem?

2. The New Jerusalem has a tree at its center, and a river of the water of life. What echoes do you see here of other biblical trees? How and why does Revelation echo Genesis, and the Passion Narrative, at the moment when the holy city is revealed?

3. Describe in what way "the whole biblical narrative comes to a point on this tree."

12

In the Fullness of Time

STEPHEN ANDREWS

THE BOOK OF REVELATION is all about end things. It is about the end of hunger and thirst (7:16). It is about the end of delay (10:6). It is about the end of Babylon (18:21–23); the end of deception (20:3). It is about the end of the first cosmos and the end of night (21:1; 22:5). It is about the end of grief, crying, and pain. It is about the end of Death (21:4). And finally, it is all about the One who is both "the beginning and the end" (21:6; 22:13).

And yet, this is not our experience. We live in a world where the grave's appetite remains unsatisfied and unremitting. We grope about in what occasionally feels like a futile attempt to find our bearings, to confirm our call, to discern the path ahead, and all the while we are drawn to the siren call of the deceivers and hawkers of earthly goods. And we continue to wait . . . and we wait . . . and we wait . . . Where is the Alpha and the Omega? The beginning and the end?

As we know, there are those who understand the Revelation of St. John the Divine to be a psychotic fantasy, expressing the repressed longings of the human spirit, or an elaborate code—keys to the details of the world's future political affairs. The biblical scholar G. B. Caird described the book as "the paradise of sectarians and fanatics."[45] While much of the imagery remains bizarre and there are details that elude deciphering, it is a work of serious theology addressed to an ancient Christian community needing a word from God. While we stand aeons and worlds apart, there is enough that *we* hold in common with our forebears that it is a word for us, too.

What is this word for us? I suggest that it is a word about time and grace.

First of all, it is a word about time. Our perception of time is conditioned by clocks. And those of us in western cultures can be dominated by an undue attention to punctuality. I was once at an international conference presided over by a Nigerian bishop. When the English delegates voiced their concerns over an agenda that had got off schedule, the bishop chided us: "You English have your watches, but we Africans have the time!"

The Book of Revelation is framed by its own understanding of time. There are seven occurrences of the term *kairos* in the book, and in each instance, it is conceived not so much in a linear fashion, but rather as a "season" or "opportunity." When the book begins and ends with the phrase "for the time is near" (1:3; 22:10), John's hearers are not expected to look at their clocks or calendars. Rather, they are meant to feel the weight of the whole of John's vision, which is carefully constructed by an elaborate patterning of images. The vision is structured in seven sections of seven elements to form a symbolic seven weeks of seven years, which itself conforms to the seven-times-seven or forty-nine-year cycle of the Jewish Jubilee. In other words,

45. Caird, *Revelation of St. John the Divine*, 2.

it is a conception of time that is ordered towards a purpose, an end, a completion, and perfection.

Moreover, in John's mind, it is clear that this completion goes beyond the symbolic cycle of the Jewish calendar. It is much more profound than a retirement party or "happily-ever-after" story. The fulfilment of time is to be found not ultimately in an event, but in a person—in the One who says "I am the Alpha and the Omega, the first and the last, the beginning and the end" (v. 13). This is an extraordinary and sweeping confession. For these words are also found at the beginning of the book (1:8), only there they are uttered by the Lord God.

In John's vision of time, then, we have the radical consummation of all things in God. He who precedes and originates all things becomes the end of all things, and all things find their meaning and purpose in him. *All* things. The story of creation and humanity's expulsion from the garden becomes a re-creation with an invitation to enter and eat from the tree of life (v. 14). The promised Messiah, both sire and son of David, is restored to the eternal throne (v. 16; cf. Isa 11:10). The prophecy of Daniel, shut until the end, is now unsealed (v. 10; cf. Dan 12:4). All things—every member of the human race, the evil and the righteous (v. 11), the filthy and the clean—will have their chosen and appointed place, and all of the redeemed will share in his new creation (v. 14–15). So John's word for us is to live in God's time, and this means trying to see all things in him. Just as the Seer sought to read his world and his Scriptures through Christ, so ought we to measure our days by his final purposes and the quality of our life in him.

And the means of this life in him? It is to be found in the book's final verse: "The grace of the Lord Jesus be with all" (v. 21). John's encouragement to live in God's time is now adorned by a bidding of grace. Throughout his vision, it is clear that his claim on the promises of God is only possible through the grace of God. It is by the grace of God that he has received words that are trustworthy and true (v. 6); it is by the grace of God that he received visits from heavenly messengers (vv. 6, 16); it is by the grace of God that he received his commission as a prophet (v. 9); it is by the grace of God that his robes are washed, his hunger sated, and his welcome assured (v. 14); it is by the grace of God that he receives the invitation of the Spirit to "come," and that he can cry "come!" in return (v. 17). And it is an invitation that comes through him to us. "Come!" say the Spirit and the bride to us. "Yes, come!" we respond.

And so we reach this encouragement: to live in God's time by God's grace. How do we do this? My counsel to you is that you continue to nurture this life in God's time by making use of God's grace through the gifts of prayer and sacrament.

Prayer is one of the chief means by which we might escape the tyranny of time and dwell, for a time, in the presence of the timeless One. The final chapter of the Revelation contains the stern command, "Worship God!" (v.9), and we are reminded of visions earlier on where the worshipful prayer of the saints filled the throne room like incense (5:8; 8:3). So we, in time, join our prayer with those who are out of time, and we find ourselves with them, engaged in timeless adoration and intercession.

But the piercing of the temporal veil goes in two directions. One of my favorite poems by the Welsh poet R. S. Thomas is called "Kneeling." As you may have guessed, it is a meditation on the theme of prayer, but its final verse is striking. The poem ends with the sentence, "The meaning is in the waiting." The meaning is in the waiting. This is Thomas's insightful way of describing the interpenetration of time with eternity. For it is in prayer that we suspend time in order to make room for the timelessness, or perhaps one might even say the "timefulness," of God to invade, illuminate, and transform.

If you are like me, you are often too demanding of God. I hear Jesus say, "I am coming soon," and lustily join the martyr's cry "How long?" I am anxious to move on, to fill the empty space with my words. But waiting is good for me. What comes to me as divine delay is often an expression of divine patience and grace, and it gives me room for reflection and repentance. Waiting in prayer is one important way of living in God's time.

There is also the sacrament. There is nothing that draws us into God's time more effectively than the Eucharist. There is a sense in which the Revelation of St. John is itself situated within a corporate act of worship. The book begins on the Lord's Day (1:10) and ends in the Eucharistic invitation: "Come!" say the Spirit and the bride, "let the thirsty come" (v. 17).

This is not simply a literary trick—a play on universal human longings. Just as the words of prayer pierce the veil separating time and eternity, so the celebration of the Lord's Supper crosses and confuses temporal boundaries. The Eucharist is both an act of remembrance—a repetition of God's saving acts in the past—and an act of anticipation, a rehearsal of the heavenly banquet that awaits. The tokens of bread and wine themselves become more than their physical species of modified wheat and grape. They become signs, signs that point to and participate in the body and blood of Christ who is himself timeless. In this way, our Communion makes all time, past and future, a reality in the present.

And so, my friends, St. John's final words to us are time and grace, while my final counsel to you is to uphold the disciplines of prayer and sacrament. For now, it is enough, it is sufficient to bring us to the threshold of the Kingdom. And in the meantime we pray, "Even so. *Marana tha!* Come, Lord Jesus!"

Revelation 22:7–21

Questions for Further Reflection

1. As you come to the end of the book of Revelation, how has your understanding of the world changed? And what are the implications of this new understanding for how you live in the world?

2. Does the description of God and Jesus Christ as the alpha and omega (Rev 22:13 and 1:8) make sense in the way you understand time? We have said that the description of the visions in Revelation as a "series of sevens" conveys something other than a linear conception of time. How does this notion of "God's time" intersect with your own? Where does it help you? Where does it challenge you?

3. The Spirit bids us, "Come" (Rev 22:17). How do you "come" to him in prayer and sacrament? And, perhaps more importantly, how does he "come" to you?

Bibliography

Associated Press. "U.N. Says World Faces Largest Humanitarian Crisis Since World War II." *The Wall Street Journal*, March 11, 2017. https://www.wsj.com/articles/u-n-says-world-faces-largest-humanitarian-crisis-since-1945–1489223549.

Barclay, William. *The Revelation of John*. 2 vols. Philadelphia: Westminster, 1976.

Barr, David. *Tales of the End: A Narrative Commentary on the Book of Revelation*. Santa Rosa, CA: Polebridge, 1998.

Boer, Harry. *The Book of Revelation*. Grand Rapids: Eerdmans, 1979.

Boring, Eugene. *Revelation*. Louisville: John Knox, 1989.

Buffy the Vampire Slayer. "Earshot." Series 3, episode 18. Written by Jane Espenson. First aired September 21, 1999.

Caird, G. B. *The Revelation of St John the Divine*. Harpers New Testament Commentaries. New York: Harper & Row, 1966.

Chonak, Richard. "No, Saint Whoever Did Not Actually Say That." *Catholic Light* blog, November 16, 2009. http://catholiclight.stblogs.org/index.php/2009/11/no-saint-whoeve/.

Collins, John J. *Apocalypse, Prophecy, and Pseudepigraphy: On Jewish Apocalyptic Literature*. Grand Rapids: Eerdmans, 2015.

Considine, J. S. "The Rider on the White Horse: Apocalypse 6:1–8." *Catholic Biblical Quarterly* 6 (1944) 406–22.

DeSilva, David A. *An Introduction to the New Testament: Contexts, Methods & Ministry Formation*. Downers Grove, IL: IVP Academic, 2004.

The Ecology Global Network. "World Birth and Death Rates." http://www.ecology.com/birth-death-rates/.

Eliot, T. S. "Ash Wednesday V." In *Collected Poems 1909–1962*, 102–3. London: Faber, 1974.

Frei, Hans W. *The Identity of Jesus Christ: The Hermeneutical Bases of Dogmatic Theology*. Eugene, OR: Wipf and Stock, 1997.

Frye, Northrop. "Revelation: After the Ego Disappears." Program 29 in *The Bible and Literature: A Personal View* (audio series). Heritage University of Toronto. http://heritage.utoronto.ca/content/bible-and-literature-personal-view-northrop-frye-program-29-revelation-after-ego-disappears.

Graves, Dan. "All Shall Be Well, and All Manner of Thing Shall Be Well." Christian History Institute blog. https://christianhistoryinstitute.org/incontext/article/julian/.

"Hawaii Panics After Alert About Incoming Missile Is Sent In Error." *New York Times*, January 13, 2018. https://www.nytimes.com/2018/01/13/us/hawaii-missile.html.

Hawking, Stephen, ed. *A Stubbornly Persistent Illusion: The Essential Scientific Works of Albert Einstein*. Philadelphia: Running, 2009.

Hoffman, Donald. "Do We See Reality As It Is?" TED 2015. https://www.ted.com/talks/donald_hoffman_do_we_see_reality_as_it_is.

Institute for Economics and Peace. *The Global Peace Index*. https://reliefweb.int/report/world/global-peace-index-2017.

Irenaeus. *Adversus Haereses*. Translated by Alexander Roberts and W. H. Rambaut. In the *Ante-Nicene Christian Library* V: *The Writings of Irenaeus*, edited by Alexander Roberts and James Donaldson. Edinburgh: Clark, 1968.

Kachur, Robert. "Getting the Last Word: British Women and the Authoritative Apocalyptic Voice (1845–1900)." PhD diss., University of Wisconsin (Madison), 1996.

Koester, Craig R. *Revelation and the End of All Things*. Grand Rapids: Eerdmans, 2001.

Lerner, Harriet. "Why That Person Who Hurt You Will Never Apologize." *Psychology Today* blog, June 11, 2017. https://www.psychologytoday.com/blog/the-dance-connection/201706/why-person-who-hurt-you-will-never-apologize.

"List of Ongoing Conflicts," Wikipedia, https://en.wikipedia.org/wiki/List_of_ongoing_armed_conflicts.

Luther, Martin. "Preface to the Revelation of St. John." In *Luther's Works*, vol. 35, *Word and Sacrament I*, edited by E. Theodore Bachmann, 398–99. Philadelphia: Fortress, 1960.

Mangina, Joseph L. *Revelation*. Grand Rapids: Brazos, 2010.

Morris, Leon. *The Revelation of St. John*. Grand Rapids: Eerdmans, 1969.

Mounce, Robert H. *The Book of Revelation*. Grand Rapids: Eerdmans, 1997.

Rossetti, Christina. *The Face of the Deep*. London: SPCK, 1893.

Schüssler Fiorenza, Elizabeth. *The Book of Revelation: Justice and Judgment*. Minneapolis: Fortress, 1985.

———. *Revelation: Vision of a Just World*. Minneapolis: Fortress, 1991.

Simeon, Charles. *Horae Homileticae: Revelation—Claude's Essay—Indexes*. Vol. 21. London: Holdsworth and Ball, 1833.

Smith, Joshua. "The Tree of Life My Soul Hath Seen." In *Common Praise*, edited by the Anglican Church of Canada, hymn 488. Toronto: Anglican Book Centre, 1998.

Turchin, Peter, et al. "Coin Hoards Speak of Population Declines in Ancient Rome." *Proceedings of the National Academy of Sciences of the United States of America* 106, no. 41 (2009) 17276–79.

Volf, Miroslav. *Exclusion and Embrace*. Nashville: Abingdon, 1996.

Wright, Ronald. *A Short History of Progress*. Toronto: Anansi, 2004.

Contributors

The Right Reverend Stephen Andrews
Principal of Wycliffe College

Terence Donaldson
Lord and Lady Coggan Professor of New Testament Studies

Alan L. Hayes
Bishops Frederick and Heber Wilkinson Professor of
Church History

Murray Henderson
Interim Chaplain at Wycliffe College

L. Ann Jervis
Professor of New Testament

David Kupp
Professor of Pastoral Theology

Joseph Mangina
Professor of Systematic Theology

Judy Paulsen
Professor of Evangelism, Director of the Institute of
Evangelism

Thomas Power
Adjunct Professor of Church History, Theological Librarian, and general editor of the Wycliffe Studies in Gospel, Church, and Culture series

Peter Robinson
Professor of Proclamation, Worship, and Ministry

Catherine Sider-Hamilton
Professor of New Testament

Marion Taylor
Professor of Old Testament

Mari Leesment is a Teaching Fellow at Wycliffe College while completing her PhD in New Testament. Her dissertation applies ancient Hellenistic Moral Psychology to Second Temple Jewish literature and the New Testament letter of James. As a Christian concerned with social injustice and environmental destruction, she finds hope and motivation in the vision of the restoration of creation and the New Jerusalem, where "the home of God is among mortals" (Rev 21:3).